799.1     Evanoff, Vlad
Ev1         A complete guide to
            fishing

# A Complete Guide to Fishing

# A Complete Guide to Fishing

Revised Edition

## Vlad Evanoff

Illustrated by the Author

Thomas Y. Crowell     New York

Designed by Al Cetta

Library of Congress Cataloging in Publication Data
Evanoff, Vlad.
    A complete guide to fishing.
    Includes index.
    SUMMARY: Explains how to use a variety of poles, tackle, baits, and lures; de-
scribes fresh and saltwater fish; and presents rules of good sportsmanship.
    1. Fishing—United States—Juvenile literature. 2. Fishes—United States—Juvenile
literature. [1. Fishing. 2. Fishes] I. Title.
SH463.E85 1981      799.1'0973      80-2251
ISBN 0-690-04090-3
ISBN 0-690-04091-1 (lib. bdg.)

3 4 5 6 7 8 9 10

# Contents

# Introduction

People have been fishing on this earth since earliest times. The early primitive humans caught fish with their bare hands and later with spears, bows and arrows, nets, crude hooks and lines. They caught fish for food. It is only in the last few hundred years that fishing has become a sport or pastime. Fish are still caught for food, but millions of people all over the world are now fishing for fun. Fishing is one of the most popular participant sports in this country, with more than 60 million anglers. Not too long ago, fishing was considered mostly a sport for men and boys. But today more and more women and girls are going fishing, and they often catch bigger fish or more fish than their male counterparts.

It is exciting to see a big fish swimming in the water, then to watch as it comes up and takes your bait or lure. The strike, the leap of a hooked fish, the run in which line is taken off the reel at great speed, the battle to land a large fish you have hooked—all of these experiences are tremendously exciting, especially when your fish is powerful or cunning.

If you catch a really big fish or record fish, you may want to have it mounted and you may win a prize in one of the many fishing contests run each year. You will surely take a photograph of a good catch or of the big one you got, and it will be a proud moment when you show the photo to your family and friends.

Fishing is a healthy pastime. It keeps you out in the open for hours, breathing fresh air and getting beneficial exercise. When you wade a trout stream or walk along the beach or rocks for some distance, when you hike or ride a bicycle to a distant fishing spot, row a boat or paddle a canoe, casting your lure repeatedly, you are constantly bringing many muscles into play.

If you are tired or feel lazy, however, you can sit on the shore, in a boat, or on a dock or pier and relax all day long. You can set your own pace and fish as long and as hard as you want. There are no regulations or rules telling you how to fish or how long to fish or where to fish. You are your own boss, and everything is left entirely up to you.

Most of the fish you catch will be good to eat. And with the high price of fish these days, you can help your family with freshly caught fish. After a day of fishing there is nothing more delicious than fresh fish fried to a crisp, golden brown—especially when you caught them yourself.

Another advantage of fishing is that you can do it by yourself. Naturally, you will often go fishing with friends or with your family. But you don't need a team of a certain number of people to go fishing. You can go alone or with one friend and have just as much fun as when you are with a large group.

One of the best things about fishing is that you don't need a lot of money to take part in the sport. Of course, some kinds of fishing require expensive fishing tackle. But once you buy an outfit it will last for years. Buying or renting or chartering a boat can also be expensive. But you can also go fishing in a boat owned by a friend or relative. Or you can fish from the shore, surf, dock, or pier at little or no cost. You can walk or ride a bicycle to nearby lakes, streams or rivers, or the ocean. You can fish with an inexpensive or even a homemade rod with bait dug out of your own backyard or garden or baits found in the water or in the fields. You can even make your own fishing lure at little cost.

Fishing can also be practiced over a long season. You

can start early in the spring and continue well into the fall. Even in the winter you can go ice fishing on fresh-water lakes or fish for cod in the ocean if you live in the right surroundings. And in many of our southern states people fish for crappies, walleyes, and bass during the winter months. Of course, if you live in Florida or near other tropical or warm waters, you can fish all year round.

Not only can you fish most of the year, you can also fish throughout your life. Young people like to play baseball, basketball, or football, but as they grow older they usually lose both interest and ability. This almost never happens with fishing. Once you take up fishing you usually keep on fishing no matter how old you get. It is truly a lifetime sport.

Although luck plays a small part in fishing, there is also a great deal of skill and knowledge involved. In the long run, the person who catches the most fish is the one who knows what fishing tackle to use, which lure or baits are best and how to present them, where to find fish, and how to make them bite or strike. But nobody ever becomes perfect at fishing: there is always something new to learn.

In recent years many fishing schools have been started all over the country. If you can afford the cost and can travel to them, you can learn how to fish in a short period of time. You can also join a local fishing club and learn about fishing from the members. Or you can go out with an experienced angler and learn from him. You can also read fishing magazines and books like this one to learn more about fishing. But the best way to learn how to fish is to go out as often as you can and to spend a lot of time actually fishing.

# A
# Complete
# Guide
# to
# Fishing

# 1. Still-fishing Tackle

If you want to fish in a nearby freshwater lake, stream, or river, you don't need to have a rod or reel. You can have a lot of fun still-fishing at a cost of a few pennies. Still-fishing means fishing from shore, dock, or anchored boat. You can use almost any live or natural bait, such as a worm or minnow, put it on a hook, and drop it into the water, where it remains in one place. Millions of people go still-fishing, and it's a good way to catch many kinds of freshwater fish.

*1*

You can start still-fishing with an ordinary drop line or hand line. This can be about 50 to 100 feet of heavy cotton, linen, or nylon line wound around a stock or wood frame for convenient carrying. Tie a sinker to the end of this line. Then tie one or two hooks on short nylon monofilament leaders, and tie the leaders just above the sinker. Bait the hooks with live worms, minnows, or doughballs. Then unwind the line from the holder and coil it in a small circle on the ground. Tie the hand end of the line to a stake in the ground, or to a bush or tree. Now pick up the sinker end of the coiled line a good distance above the hooks and twirl it around and around; then release it and let the sinker and baited hooks (the rig) fly out into the water. Be careful of the hooks when you twirl so as not to hook yourself. Then after you throw the hand line out, let the sinker and baited hooks lie still on the bottom. When you get a bite, jerk the line quickly in order to set the hook and then pull in the fish.

Drop lines or hand lines are best when you are fishing for big fish such as carp and catfish. For more sport with the smaller fish, a pole is often used. If you live in the country, find a good, straight sapling for a fishing pole. You can make this sapling lighter by removing the bark and then letting the pole dry. A sapling cut from a birch or alder tree is best, but any young, straight, thin tree that you find in the fields or woods will do.

If you live in a city or town or near a shopping area,

you can buy a bamboo or cane pole in almost any fishing tackle or hardware store. A pole about 10 or 12 feet long is the best length. Longer ones are usually too heavy. Cane poles come in one piece or in two or three sections. A one-piece pole is excellent if you live near the water where you fish and can walk with the pole to the fishing spot. But if you must travel to reach the fishing spot, a cane pole that comes in sections is easier to carry on a bicycle or in a car, train, or bus. A pole that comes in sections is also better for storing in a small space such as a closet.

You can also buy fiberglass poles for still-fishing, but these are somewhat more expensive. Fiberglass poles are made of hollow tubes that slide in and out like the sections of a telescope. They measure 4 or 5 feet when closed and open to 10, 12, 14, or even 20 feet when ready for fishing. Such hollow glass poles are very strong and light and will last a long time.

In addition to the cane or glass pole, you need some fishing line. Almost any thin, strong line can be used, but the nylon monofilament line is best. It is difficult for fish to see this line, and it gets more bites. The mono-line can test anywhere from 10 to 25 pounds in strength, depending on how big a fish you expect to catch. The line should be as long as the pole, and you tie one end of the line to the tip of the pole.

Next you need a float or bobber, and you can buy one or two made of plastic at any fishing tackle store. But you can easily make your own by using a cork bottle

hole

matchstick or other stick →

fishing line through hole

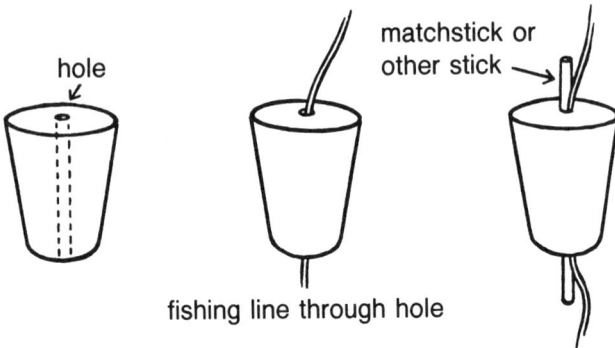

**Making bobber or float from cork bottle stopper**

stopper and a wooden matchstick or any other small, thin stick. Make a hole through the center of the cork from one end to the other with a nail or an ice pick. Then push the end of the line through this hole with a stick. Slide the cork up the line about 4 or 5 feet and push the matchstick through the hole to keep the cork from sliding down the line. (See the drawing.)

To complete the still-fishing outfit, you need hooks. The parts of a hook are called the shank, the bend, the eye, the barb, and the point. Hooks come in different sizes, shapes, and bends, depending on the fish to be

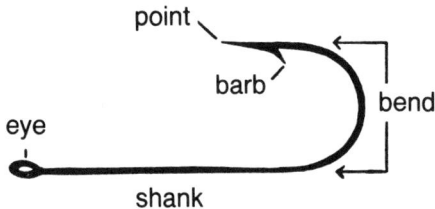

point

barb

bend

eye

shank

**Parts of a hook**

caught. For small fish, for example, a hook with thin wire is strong enough. For big fish you need a heavier wire, which is often flattened or forged to give it still more strength. For freshwater fishing the most popular patterns of hooks are the Sproat, the Aberdeen, the Carlisle, and the Round Bend. Another very good hook is the Eagle Claw, which can be used for most freshwater fish. It has a rolled-in point shaped like an eagle's talon or claw. This helps to hook and hold a fish securely.

The size of the hook you use will depend on the fish you expect to catch. As a general rule, the small fish with small mouths require smaller-size hooks than the bigger fish with large mouths. The best sizes to buy are Nos. 8, 6, 4, 2, and 1 for such small fish as sunfish, yellow perch, crappies, white bass, suckers, and trout. For bass, pickerel, carp, and catfish sizes, Nos. 1/0, 2/0, and 3/0 are often required. You can buy hooks loose by the dozen, or in boxes of 100 of one size, or you can get a whole box of assorted hooks in different sizes.

Tie the hook directly to the end of the line. A good knot to use for tying a hook to a line or leader is the improved clinch knot, shown in the illustration.

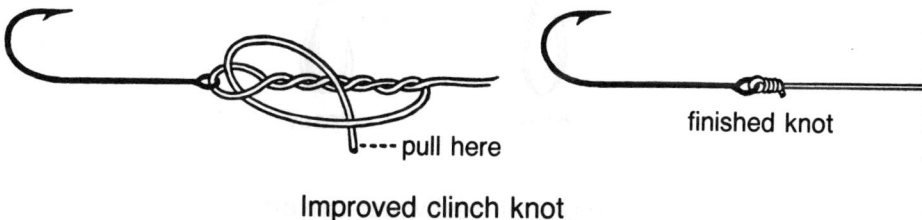

pull here

finished knot

Improved clinch knot

The most important thing to remember about hooks is that the points should always be sharp. Feel the point with your thumb, and if it feels dull, sharpen it with a small file or sharpening stone. If a hook is rusted, throw it away. Rusty hooks are weak and may break when you hook a big fish.

For most still-fishing with bait you can add a small split-shot sinker a foot or a bit more above the hook. If the current is strong or if you want to cast the bait out farther, you can get a clincher or rubber-core sinker and put it on your line. If you fish for catfish or carp, you can use a dipsey or bank or egg sinker to keep the bait lying on the bottom of the river or lake.

For still-fishing you will also need live baits such as worms, minnows, frogs, crayfish, grasshoppers, crickets, other insects, and doughballs. These will be covered later on in more detail.

You usually don't need a big tackle box to hold your

split-shot          clincher

bank                dipsey

Types of freshwater sinkers

still-fishing tackle. An old tobacco or other small tin box, a wood box, or a plastic container will hold all your hooks, sinkers, and extra line so that they can be carried in your pocket. You can also buy a small transparent plastic box with many compartments to hold your tackle. If you fish from a boat or stay in one spot all day, you can use a larger tackle box. These boxes can be bought in any sporting goods store, or you can make one yourself. We'll show you how later in this book.

# 2. Spinning Tackle

Since its introduction from Europe soon after World War II, spinning, or spin casting, has become the most popular method of freshwater fishing in this country. This is partly because spinning tackle makes casting easy. Spin casting is also less tiring than either bait casting or fly casting, and there are no "backlashes" or "birdnests" such as those found in bait casting. The rods, reels, and lines are much lighter, and you can cast all day without getting tired. And you can cast from any position or spot: standing up, sitting down, with steep banks behind you or trees overhead, from shore, or from a boat.

Spinning tackle also catches more fish both for the beginner and for the expert angler. The thin, almost invisible lines used in spinning easily fool fish. In addition, you use smaller, lighter lures with spinning tackle than with bait-casting tackle, and these fool many fish that would avoid the larger, heavier lures. Therefore, if you can afford only one freshwater fishing outfit, you will do well with a spinning rod and reel.

## Rods

Most spinning rods are made of fiberglass, hollow or solid. In recent years new rods have appeared made from graphite and Boron. These are superior to fiberglass rods, but they are also much more expensive. Solid fiberglass spinning rods are cheaper than most rods and are very strong. But they are a bit heavier and haven't the superior action of the hollow glass rod. So a hollow rod is therefore preferable.

For general, or "all-around," fishing, a medium-weight spinning rod is a good buy. This rod runs from 6 to 7 feet long and can cast lures or sinkers weighing from ¼ to ⅝ ounces, which include most of the spinning lures. You can use this rod for fishing in lakes, streams, and rivers for most freshwater fish.

If you plan to fish mostly for trout in small streams or for small fish such as sunfish or other panfish in small ponds, a light spinning rod is better. This rod will run from 5½ to 6 feet long and cast lures weighing from ⅛ to ½ ounce. There are also "ultralight" rods, which are even lighter, and they will cast the lightest lures and make a small fish feel like a big one on the end of the line.

If you will fish in big lakes or wide rivers for large fish such as big bass, pike, muskellunge, steelhead, salmon, freshwater striped bass, big carp, or catfish, you should get a heavy spinning rod from 6 to 8 feet long. Such a rod with a stiff action can cast lures from ½ to 1 ounce. It is also best when fishing on a rocky bottom or in heavy lily pads or weeds.

Spinning rods come mostly in one or two separate sections. A one-piece rod is a bit stronger and has better action, but is more difficult to store or carry. A two-piece spinning rod is handier and preferred by most anglers.

## Reels

The reel is the most important part of spinning equipment. You can save money by buying a cheaper spinning rod, but get the best reel you can afford. It will give you less trouble, last much longer, and be less expensive in the end.

There are two main types of spinning reels: the open-faced reel and the closed-faced reel. The closed-faced spinning reel has a housing that fits over the end of the spool and hides the line from view. The line comes out

Closed-faced spin-casting reel

of a small hole in front of this housing. You press buttons or levers to release the line when casting. This reel is called either a spin-casting or push-button reel. This reel is very simple to use and is the most popular with beginners. This reel is also used with special spin-casting rods similar to the bait-casting rods described in the next chapter.

The other reel is the open-faced spinning reel, which has an exposed spool so that the line is visible. A "bail" pickup catches the line and guides it to a roller that winds it back on the reel spool after a cast. The more modern open-faced reels have a "skirted" spool that prevents the line from getting in behind the spool.

Any of the two reels described above will enable you to cast far and catch fish. The closed-faced, or spin-casting, reel is the easiest and cheapest to use and is bought by novice or beginning anglers. It works simply and gives less trouble than the open-faced spinning reel. One advantage of the open-faced reel is that it has a larger spool than the closed-faced, or spin-casting, reel and holds more line. So you can usually make longer casts with the open-faced reel. The open-faced reel is also better when fighting big fish that take a lot of line off the reel. And the open-faced reel is best for use with very light lines. You can change spools more easily, so that if you have two or three spools with different strength lines, you are prepared to fish for all kinds of freshwater fish in many waters.

If you are just starting to fish or plan to fish only a few times a year, you can get a closed-faced, or spin-casting, reel. But if you plan to fish often and in different waters and for different kinds of fish, an open-faced spinning reel will be more useful.

## Lines

The closed-faced, or spin-casting, reel usually comes with the line already wound on the spool. The open-faced reel comes empty, but some fishing tackle stores will fill the reel with line at a slight extra charge. The line used on spinning reels is usually monofilament nylon or other synthetic and is called monoline. It is almost invisible, wears well, and casts smoothly.

Spinning lines usually come on 100-to-300-yard spools or on larger bulk spools holding several hundred yards. Most freshwater spinning reels will hold up to 200 or 250 yards of line. So find out how much your reel holds before buying the line. The best and cheapest way to buy lines is on a bulk spool or ¼-pound spool, which holds enough line to fill your reel two or three times.

The size and strength of the line are important. The thinner the line, the farther you can cast. If you have a light spinning rod and fish mostly for trout, small bass, or panfish, you can use a line testing 3 or 4 pounds. With a medium-weight spinning rod you can use lines testing 6 pounds. For the heavier spinning rods and when fishing in waters filled with weeds, lily pads, logs, or rocks, a line testing from 8 to 15 pounds may be needed.

It is a good idea to buy one or two extra spools for your spinning reels wound with different strength lines. In this way you can change to a lighter or heavier line to suit the fishing conditions.

Although you can buy the spinning rod, reel, and line separately, you can often save some money and get a more balanced spinning outfit by buying the complete set. Many stores have sales where you can buy the entire outfit at one time. Or you can buy a complete kit in a package or box that includes the rod, reel, line, and perhaps a few lures. It is best not to buy the cheapest rods, reels, lines, or kits on sale. Buy one in the medium-priced range, and you will get a higher quality outfit that will give you less trouble.

When you go spin fishing, certain extras or accessories will make your fishing trip more comfortable and successful. If you fish a trout stream, you'll need a pair of rubber hip boots in shallow water or a pair of waders reaching your waist or armpits for deeper rivers.

Because you cannot lift a heavy fish into a boat or onto a steep bank with the thin lines used in spin fishing, you will need a landing net. There are many kinds of landing nets—small ones for trout and larger ones for big fish.

You also will need a fairly large tackle box to hold the different lures and other small tackle. Such boxes come in various sizes and styles and are made from metal, fiberglass, or plastic. The metal, fiberglass, and plastic boxes are the most popular because they are strong and light. Tackle boxes usually have swinging or cantilever trays with many compartments for holding a lot of fishing lures.

You can also make your own tackle box from wood. You can buy the wood in any lumberyard. The boards should be about ¼ or ⅜ inch thick. Plywood, which is lighter and thinner than regular wood, is a good material. A handy size for such a tackle box is 15 inches long, 6 inches wide, and 6 inches high. There should be a tray inside that can be lifted out and is divided into compartments to hold the fishing lures. Two strips of wood, one at each end of the box on the inside, will keep this tray from falling to the bottom and give you some extra space underneath. You also need two hinges to attach the cover to the box, a hasp or lock to keep the box closed, and a handle for carrying, which is attached

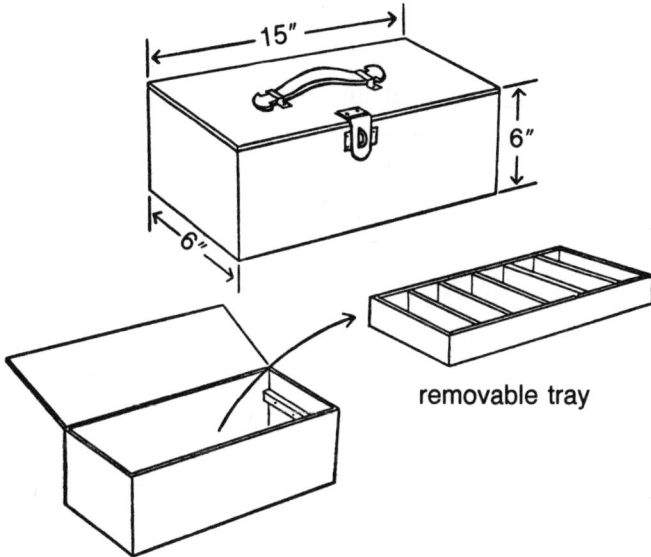

15"

6"

6"

removable tray

Homemade tackle box

to the cover. You can buy these parts in most hardware stores. After you have finished making the box, you should give it at least two coats of either paint or varnish.

Most of the hooks and sinkers used for spin casting are the same as those described in chapter 1. The lures you will need will be covered in chapter 6.

## How to Spin Cast

Before casting with a spinning rod and reel, make sure the spool is properly filled with line, neither too full nor too spare. If it is too full, the line will jump off the spool; if it is too spare you won't be able to cast any distance.

You can practice casting from the shore of a lake or river. If you have no water nearby, you can cast over a lawn or field. For practice casting, you should buy a small rubber casting weight found in any fishing tackle store. Or you can make a casting weight yourself from a round peice of wood or dowel and a screw eye. Simply screw the eye into the wood and tie your line to it. A newspaper or large piece of cardboard spread on the grass will make a good target to hit.

To cast, hold the rod with the right hand above the reel, which hangs under the handle. The thumb rests on top of the rod handle with two fingers in front of the reel support or leg. The other two fingers are behind this support. (See illustration.)

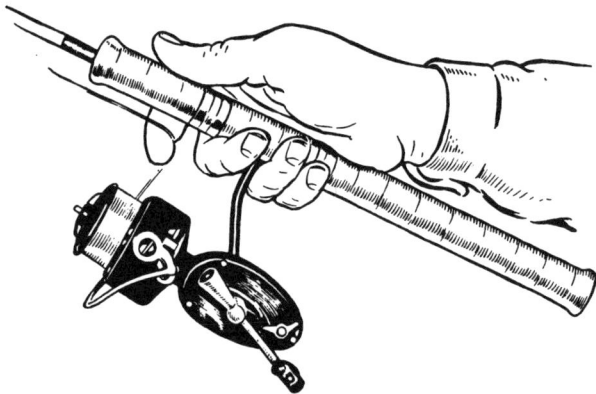

Holding open-faced spinning rod and reel

If you are casting with an open-faced spinning reel, push the bail, or wire, which picks up the line after a cast, out of the way with your left hand. The forefinger of your right hand holds the line after it has been removed from the roller on the reel. The casting weight should hang a few inches from the tip of the rod.

Now hold the rod pointing toward the target with the tip raised at an angle above the horizontal (at about the 10 o'clock position on a clock face). Then bring the rod up and back fast until it is directly over your head. Now start the forward cast immediately. This forward movement should be a fast, snappy throw. The rod will bend backward under the weight on the end of the line, which is still behind it. When the rod reaches a position in front of you, release the line from your forefinger and let the casting weight shoot out in front of you. When the weight reaches the target, or the spot you want to hit, drop your forefinger on the reel spool edge to stop the cast.

If you find the casting weight or lure going too high into the air, it means you released the line from your finger too soon. If the weight or lure drops right in front of you, then you released it too late. It will take only a short time to correct your timing so that the lure or weight is released at the proper moment and travels above the ground or water straight toward the target.

Casting with a closed-faced, or spin-casting, type of reel is very similar, except that instead of holding the line on your forefinger, you merely depress the button on the reel. Holding the button down, you bring the rod back, then forward, releasing the button to send the weight or lure on its way.

If you practice casting with your spin-casting, or spinning, reel and rod every day for a half hour or so, in a few days you will have enough accuracy to begin to catch fish.

# 3. Bait-Casting Tackle

Before spinning tackle became popular, most freshwater anglers used bait-casting tackle. Casting with a bait-casting reel is more difficult, and many people get discouraged when the line on the spool snarls or backlashes. But if you practice long enough you will find that this tackle is practical for many types of freshwater fishing.

You can cast more accurately with bait-casting tackle than with spinning tackle. This is especially valuable when you fish near shore and have to cast around overhanging trees or near stumps, logs, lily pads, and other tight spots. Bait-casting tackle is also better for hooking and holding big fish such as pike, muskellunge, lake trout, salmon, or freshwater striped bass. Using it, you can slow down a fish or turn it away from obstructions in the water more successfully. Finally, bait-casting tackle is better than spinning tackle for trolling (letting the lure out behind the boat).

## Rods

Formerly bait-casting rods were made of anything from bamboo to steel, but today the hollow fiberglass rods are the most popular. Some of the more expensive bait-casting rods are also made from graphite and Boron. Bait-casting rods vary from 4 to 6½ feet in length. They come in different actions from very limber to very stiff. Limber rods are best for light lures and small fish, while the stiffer rods are used for heavy lures, big fish, and for fishing in weeds or around logs and stumps. The so-called worm rod is a heavy, stiff rod used to fish plastic worms as lures.

A medium-action bait-casting rod from 5 to 6 feet long is the most practical for general, or all-around, fishing and will cast lures from ⅜ to ¾ ounces—the weights of most lures made for bait casting. This rod is ideal for big trout, pickerel, walleyes, catfish, carp, and for most bass and panfish.

The heavy bait-casting outfit runs from 4½ to 6 feet

and has a stiffer action for casting lures from ⅝ to 1 ounce or a bit heavier. This rod is best for big fish with tough mouths and in rough fishing situations in weeds or around other obstructions. It can be used for big bass, salmon, freshwater striped bass, lake trout, pike, muskellunge, big carp, and big catfish.

There are also light-action bait-casting rods, but for casting light lures for small fish, you'll do just as well with a light spinning outfit.

Bait-casting rods are made in one or two pieces. Some of these rods separate at the middle, while others have a single-piece rod and come apart at the handle. Nowadays most bait-casting rods are made with a pistol grip for more comfortable holding and less tiring casting.

## Reels

The reel is the most important part of your bait-casting outfit. A well-made, smooth-working reel allows you to cast easily and will last for many years. In recent years the better bait-casting reels have become expensive. Here again, do not buy the cheapest reel made. Get one in the middle-class range.

A bait-casting reel has a revolving spool that turns during the cast. You can control the cast and stop it with your thumb once you learn how to use it. Most bait-casting reels today also have a level-wind device— a metal finger that moves back and forth in front of the reel, spreading the line evenly as it is wound on the spool. In this way the line never bunches up unevenly on the spool, and you have less trouble in casting. Many bait-casting reels also have antibacklash devices. These prevent the reel spool from revolving too fast during the cast. Most backlashes or line tangles occur when the spool revolves faster than the line can go out. An antibacklash device applies tension that slows the spool down especially toward the end of the cast. But even with such reels you will control the cast better if you thumb the side of the spool and some of the line during the cast.

Many bait-casting reels today also have free-spool buttons or levers that keep the handle from turning during a cast. And many reels also have a star drag or other control that enables a fish to take line only under tension. This is especially useful when fighting big fish that make long runs or pull very hard.

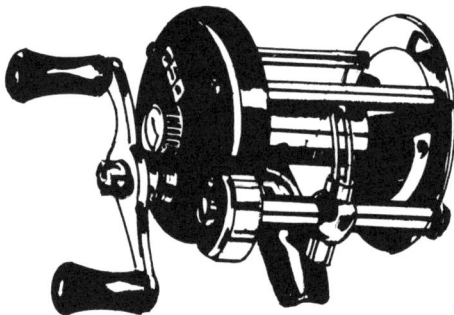

Bait-casting reel

# Lines

Before synthetic lines were developed, bait-casting lines were usually made of silk. Today they are made of braided nylon or Dacron, or anglers use the same monofilament lines used for spinning. Braided lines are easier to use than monolines and cause less trouble during a cast, especially for beginning anglers.

Bait-casting lines come on spools of 50, 100, or 200 yards. Monolines come on such small spools and also on larger bulk spools holding more line. They come in different strengths ranging from 10 to 25 pounds, which are usually used with bait-casting outfits. The lighter lines from 12 to 15 pounds are best to use with the medium-action bait-casting rod. The heavier lines from 18-to-25-pound test are used with the heavier bait-casting outfits and for big fish.

When you buy a spool of bait-casting line, you must transfer it to the reel. To do this, take the end of the line and run it through the level-winding guide and tie it to the reel spool. Then take the spool of line and push a pencil through the hole, which is usually covered by the paper label.

Then let another person hold the pencil on both ends while you crank the handle of the reel to wind on the line. The person who holds the line and pencil should apply some tension by pressing against the sides of the line spool with the fingers.

# Leaders

If you are using a braided or Dacron bait-casting line on your reel, you should attach a short "shocker" leader on the end of the line. For this, nylon monofilament about the same strength or a bit stronger than the main fishing line should be used. In other words, if the line on the reel tests 15 pounds, you can use a 15- or 18-pound test monoleader on the end. This monoleader can be about 3 or 4 feet long. On the end of this leader you can attach a snap swivel for changing lures quickly. If you fish mainly for pike or muskellunge, you can use a short wire leader a few inches long on the end of the leader. These two fish have sharp teeth and can bite through lines or monoleaders.

For bait casting you also need a tackle box to hold lures and other accessories such as sinkers, leaders, snaps, swivels, and hooks. You can buy a metal or plastic box made especially to hold bait-casting lures and tackle. Or you can make your own following the instructions in chapter 2. However, for bait-casting lures, which are bigger than spinning lures, you can make the tackle box and compartments somewhat larger in size.

You also need a big landing net if you fish from a boat, a steep bank, or shore. Get one with a fairly long handle so that you can reach out and scoop up the fish easily and don't have to lean too far over the side of the boat.

You also need a wide variety of bait-casting lures such as those described in chapter 6.

## How to Bait Cast

After you assemble your bait-casting rod, reel, and line and tie a practice weight or lure on the end of your line, you are ready to cast. In bait casting, the rod is sighted at the target and held with the reel handles facing up. The weight or lure hangs a few inches from the rod tip and the thumb is held against the side of the reel spool and some of the line. Now, using only the wrist, bring the rod up and back over your head. You will feel the weight or lure bend the rod tip still farther back. Then start the forward cast immediately and bring the rod down in front of you, at the same time removing your thumb from the reel spool to send the lure on its way. As the lure moves out, put your thumb back on the reel spool and line to regulate the speed of the revolving spool. Too much pressure will slow it down and shorten your cast. Too little pressure may

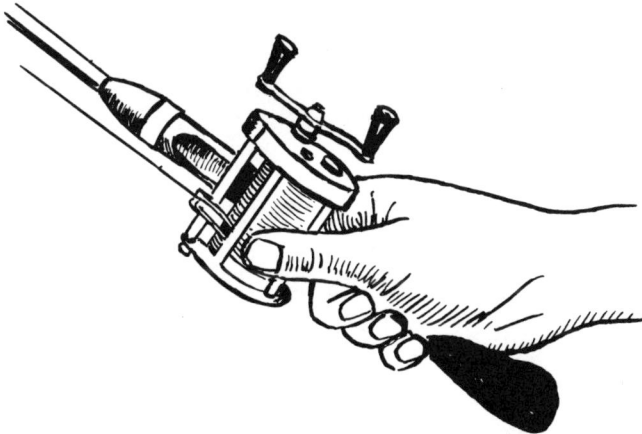

Holding bait-casting rod and reel

allow the spool to overrun and cause a backlash or snarl. When the lure reaches the target, stop the cast with your thumb.

A good bait caster educates the thumb so that it keeps the spool revolving at the right speed during the entire cast. This takes practice, of course, but after a while it becomes automatic. If you have an antiback-lash device on your reel, you can adjust this to match the weight of the lure being used, and this will help you to cast better.

# 4. Fly-Casting Tackle

Fishing with a fly rod is one of the most enjoyable ways of catching any fish, but especially when it comes to catching trout. It is also ideal for panfish since even the smallest fish puts up a good fight when caught on a fly rod. Many freshwater anglers would rather catch one fish on a fly rod than a dozen on any other type of fishing tackle.

Some people hesitate to try fly-fishing because they believe it is difficult to learn. This is not true, since you can learn how to cast with a fly rod in a short time and can start catching fish almost from the beginning. However, it does take time to learn how to use the artificial flies or lures with a fly rod. But if you go fly-fishing often, this knowledge and skill will gradually be acquired so that you'll start catching your share of fish.

## Rods

Fly rods were formerly made from split bamboo, and a few expensive ones are still being made from this material. But most fly rods today are made from hollow fiberglass, graphite, Boron, or a combination of these materials. Some expert anglers claim that bamboo fly rods are better than glass rods, but the beginner is better off if he or she buys a hollow glass fly rod. It is stronger than bamboo, will last longer, and requires less care.

Fly rods are thin and flexible and run from 7 to 12 feet or even longer. The shorter, lighter rods are used for small streams, short casts, small fish, and dry fly-fishing. The longer, heavier rods are used for big rivers and lakes, long casts, and big fish such as the larger trout, bass, salmon, and steelhead. They are also used for casting bigger, bulkier lures such as streamers and bass bugs.

The beginner will find that the lighter fly rods are easier to cast with for long periods of time, so your first rod should be about 8 feet long. Make sure it is a trout rod with dry-fly action. Then it will handle dry flies better, but can still be used to fish with other types of flies.

Fly rods come in two or three sections. Three-section rods are shorter when taken apart and are easier to carry or store. But two-section rods are only slightly longer, and it really doesn't matter which one you get.

You can buy a good hollow fiberglass fly rod that will last you a long time for about $20 to $30. You can also spend a bit less and still get a fly rod you can use, but if you buy too cheap a rod you will become dissatisfied with it after a while. If you buy the best you can afford, you will enjoy using it for many years. Later on when you have more money and become more skilled at fly-fishing, you may want to get a more expensive rod made of bamboo or graphite or Boron.

Make sure that the fly rod you buy has a hard or rigid case, such as a tube, where the rod can be stored when not in use, since the thin tip section of a fly rod is easily broken. If the rod has no such case, you can buy one to fit in most fishing tackle stores.

## Reels

Fly reels are not used in casting, but merely hold the fly line that is not being used. Two kinds of fly-fishing reels are used: the single-action and the automatic. The single-action reel is light and holds a lot of line. The line is stripped off the reel by hand and is reeled back on by hand. There is a handle for winding the line on the reel.

Single-action fly reels are preferred by most expert anglers going after big fish that make long runs and are fought directly from the reel. So if you plan to fish mostly for salmon, steelhead, freshwater stripers, or other big, fast fish that make long runs, get one of the larger, more expensive single-action fly reels. But for the smaller trout and panfish, a cheaper, smaller single-action fly reel costing from $8 to $15 will serve the purpose.

The automatic fly reel is heavier and holds less line than the single-action type. However, it is somewhat easier to use, since the slack line is taken up automatically and spooled back on the reel by just pressing a lever. Such a reel is more expensive than a single-action fly reel and costs anywhere between $15 and $30. In the beginning, it really doesn't make too much difference which reel you buy since the reel isn't as important in fly-fishing as the rod or the line.

single-action                automatic

**Fly-rod reels**

## Lines

In bait casting or spinning, the weight of the lure carries the line to the spot you want to hit. In fly casting, the weight of the line carries the lure or fly to the target, since most flies are very light. Thus it is very important to get the right size of fly line to fit your fly rod. There are three basic kinds of lines used in fly-fishing: the level line, the double-tapered line, and the three-diameter line. The level line is of equal diameter along its entire length. This is the cheapest fly line you can buy and a good one for a beginner. It costs about $5 or $6, and in addition to being an excellent line for practice casting, it can be used for many types of fly-fishing. You can use wet flies, streamers, bucktails, and live bait with this line.

The double-tapered fly line is of equal diameter along the center, then becomes thinner toward both ends. This is a good general casting line for most fly-fishing, except when you are using big, heavy flies or bass bugs. It is the best line to use for fishing with dry flies. Its advantage is that the thin, light end of the line makes less disturbance on the surface of the water and is less visible. A good double-tapered fly line will cost you anywhere between $10 and $15.

The three-diameter fly line is also called the torpedo line, bug-taper line, and weight-forward line. This line has a short, thin, tapered section in front, followed by a heavy, thick section (or head) and then by a long, thinner section of line called the running or shooting line. The heavy section near the front of the line carries the thinner section that follows it for great distances. The three-diameter fly line is therefore designed for making long casts and for casting heavy or bulky lures such as bass bugs, big streamers, and bucktails. It is best for casting on big rivers or lakes, especially into a wind and where you need distance. It is also the line to use when fishing for bass and steelhead. The weight-forward, or three-diameter, line also runs from about $10 to $20 in price.

Fly lines come in many different weights or thicknesses to match the rod you are using. If you get too light a line you won't be able to cast any distance. Fly lines are numbered and lettered, such as L4F, DT5F, WF7F, or WF8S. These and other numbers give you the type of line it is, its weight, and whether it is a floating or sinking line.

For most beginners a level or double-tapered floating fly line is the best one to get when fishing for trout, bass, or panfish. Later on, you can get one or two of the other kinds of lines to enable you to fish under a greater variety of fishing conditions.

Some fly rods have the number of the correct fly line to use printed on the rod itself near the handle. If not, the manufacturer's catalog will tell you what line matches the fly rod you have. You can also ask an experienced flycaster to help you choose the proper fly line for your fly rod. Or you can buy the fly line at the same time you get the fly rod, and then the tackle dealer will recommend the right line to get.

# Leaders

Since fly lines are heavy, thick, and very visible, and fall on the water with some disturbance, they easily frighten fish. You therefore need a nylon leader at the end of the line. Your fly or other lure is then tied to the end of this leader. Nylon leaders come either level or tapered. The level leaders are of equal diameter and strength and can be used for fly casting with bass bugs, streamers, or bucktails or for fishing with live bait. But for casting small flies you will need tapered leaders. These are thin at the end where the fly is tied and get heavier and thicker toward the end where the fly line is attached. The leaders come in lengths from 6 to 12 feet. In the beginning you will find it easier to cast with 6-, 7-, or 7½-foot leaders. After you learn how to cast well, you can use the longer leaders.

Nylon fly leaders can be bought already made up in almost any fishing tackle store. If you buy such leaders get the "knotless" kind, which taper from the thin to the thick end without any knots in between. However, if you want to save some money, you can buy nylon leader material (mono–fishing line) in coils or on spools and tie your own fly-fishing leaders. It is best to buy several coils or spools of line in different strengths and then tie your own tapered fly leaders. At the tippet, or lightest end, the leader will test about 2 pounds and then increase in strength and diameter to 20 or even 30 pounds at the butt end, the thickest part where the leader is tied to the fly line.

In the beginning you can make a simple tapered fly

leader by cutting 16-inch lengths of 2-, 6-, 10-, 15-, and 20-pound-test nylon leader material or monoline and tying them together. This will give you a fairly short tapered fly leader suitable for general fly-fishing. Later on, you can experiment and tie up different lengths and combinations of leaders to match your fly rod, the line, and the fishing you do.

The best knot for tying fly leaders is the blood knot, which is shown in the drawing. You can also use the surgeon's knot, also shown. For attaching the thick end of the fly leader to the thin end of the fly line, you use the nail knot, illustrated here.

To tie the nail knot, first get a nail and lay the end of the fly line against it. Then make several turns with the end of the fly leader as shown in step 1, running the end of this leader through the turns. The turns are then pulled up close as in step 2. In step 3 the turns must be held between thumb and forefinger to keep them in place while the ends are pulled tight. In step 4 the ends are cut off close.

## Accessories

The fly angler fishing in streams for trout needs a pair of hip boots or waders. Boots are good enough for small, shallow streams, but for the large, deep rivers a pair of waist-high waders are much better. You also need a creel to keep fish after they are caught. Two types are made for trout fishers: the willow creel, which is rather bulky and heavy, and the canvas or

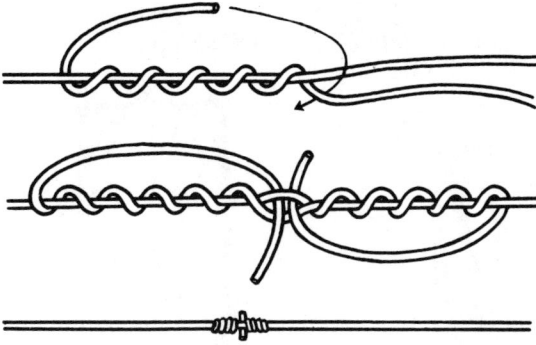

Blood knot

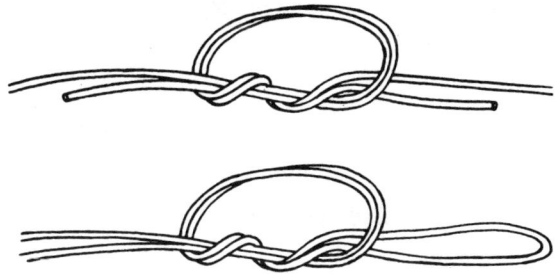

Surgeon's knot

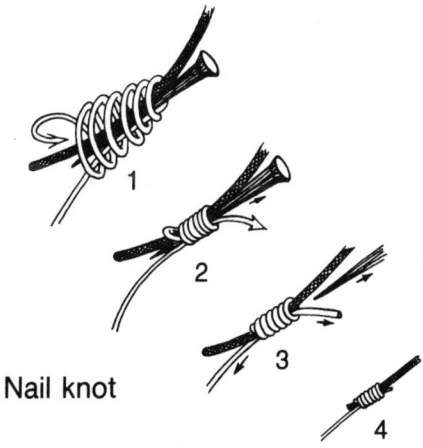

Nail knot

Hip boot and waders

plastic creel, which is lighter and fits flat against the body.

You also need a small landing net for netting a trout that has been hooked and brought in close. The best kind of landing net is one with an elastic cord that stretches and goes around your shoulder or is attached to a snap on your jacket or vest. As in other types of fishing you also need a small tackle box or two to hold the various flies and other lures. A small transparent plastic box can be used or one of the small metal fly boxes with separate compartments or clips for holding flies. To complete your fly-fishing outfit you need an assortment of artificial flies. These will be described in chapter 6.

# How to Fly-Cast

You can practice fly-casting on a lawn or on the water. The rod, reel, and line should be assembled and the fly line threaded through the guides on the rod. Although you can practice casting with the fly line alone, it's a good idea to tie on a 6- or 7-foot tapered fly leader with a small bright fly or piece of white rag on the end of this leader. If you are using a regular fly, clip off the point and barb with a pair of cutting pliers so that you don't get hooked while you are learning how to cast.

Grasp the cork grip on the rod with your right hand, resting the thumb on top. (See illustration below.) Then strip some line off the reel with your left hand and wave the rod forward and backward to let it slip through the guides. Keep the fly line moving through

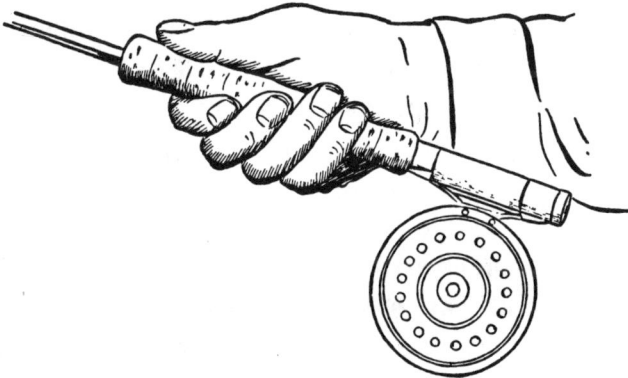

Holding fly rod

the air until you have about 20 feet of line past the tip of the rod. Then let it fall on the grass or water in front of you.

When the line is straight in front of you on the lawn or water, point the rod at the target at an angle with the tip higher than the handle you are holding. Now with a sharp upward and backward motion of your wrist and forearm, pick the line up and let it rise above and behind you. Try to see if you can make the line sail straight up into the air directly above your head. It won't get there, but it will stay high in the air, which is what you want. Stop the rod when it reaches a point at 12 o'clock, directly over your head. The pull of the line will take your rod back a bit more, but don't let it go much farther than a point at 1 o'clock. The line will start unrolling in a loop behind you, and when it is almost straight (you will feel the pull on your rod tip), you start the forward cast. Push the rod in front of you with your wrist. As the line shoots forward, follow it with your rod tip. Then let the line fall in a straight line in front of you on the lawn or the water.

This is the overhead cast and the one that you will use for most of your fishing. There are other casts that will be easy after you have learned this first overhead cast. It takes practice to become a good flycaster, so try to set aside at least a half hour every day for some casting practice. After a matter of days—at the most two to three weeks—you will be able to cast a fly far enough to catch fish.

# 5. Freshwater Baits

Natural, or live, baits catch many fish each year in fresh water. A good angler must know all about these natural baits: where and how to obtain the bait, how to keep it alive until it is used, how to hook the bait so that it stays alive and attracts fish. Finally the angler must know how to present the bait to the fish in the best way.

# Worms

The most popular bait for freshwater fishing is the earthworm, or angleworm. Worms are popular because they are usually easy to get or buy, and the freshwater fish bite on them readily. Two kinds of these worms are generally used for fishing. The first is the big night crawler, which may grow to 8 or 10 inches in length. It is found in lawns, fields, and gardens, deep in the soil. Night crawlers are too deep to dig out with an ordinary shovel, but they come to the top at night, especially after a heavy rain. You can go out at night with a flashlight and grab them before they can escape into their holes. You have to walk very softly, because the big worms can feel the vibrations through the ground. They are also sensitive to a strong light, so you should shine your flashlight a little to the side of the worm.

The other worm used in fishing is the common earthworm, or garden hackle, which is smaller than the night crawler. It lives in rich, well-moistened soil such as that found in gardens, and can be dug out with a garden fork or shovel. Worms are always easier to find when the ground is wet, since when the ground is too dry they burrow deep in search of moisture. Always try to dig your worms after a heavy rain. Some anglers dig a lot of worms in the spring when the soil is damp and keep them for future use.

When worms are plentiful in the ground, it is a good idea to dig as many as you can and keep them in a big wooden box filled with earth and rotted leaves or grass.

Keep this box in the shade or a cool cellar. If you keep them outside, cover the box so that the rain will not soak the soil. The worms can be fed cornmeal, bread crumbs, chicken mash, and almost any other vegetable remains. Mix these well into the top of the soil for best results. You can also spill some water over the soil every few days to keep it moist. Worms kept this way in a big box will live for a long time and can be dug up to take on a fishing trip as needed.

When you go fishing you can keep the worms in a small can or plastic box. Fill it partly with earth and put the worms into it. If you keep this container out of the hot sun, the worms will stay alive for an entire day.

There are many ways to put a worm on a hook, depending on what kind of fish you want to catch. When fishing for trout you hook the worm once through the middle. If you are fishing for small panfish such as sunfish, yellow perch, or rock bass, you hook a small worm one, two, or three times, allowing both ends to wriggle. For bass one whole night crawler can be hooked once or twice through the middle, or you can put two or three smaller worms on the hook. When

**Hooking worms**

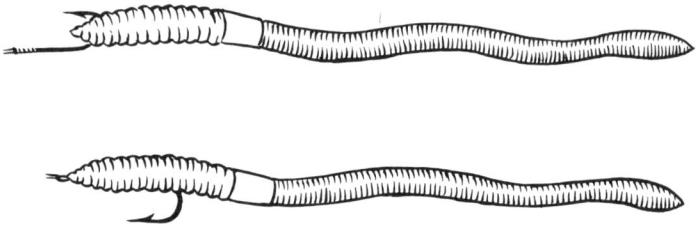

Hooking night crawlers

drifting deep with a sliding sinker rig for bass or walleyes, you can hook a whole, big night crawler in the head with a small hook.

## Minnows

Minnows are small fish that are widely used for bait in fresh water. There are many kinds of minnows, such as chubs, shiners, dace, bluntnose, and fatheads. You can catch your own minnows by using seines, umbrella nets, or minnow traps. A seine is a long net that is dragged through the water by two people. An umbrella net is a square or round net that is tied to strings and is lowered into the water. When the minnows swim over it, it is quickly raised. To attract minnows you can scatter some bread crumbs over the net. A minnow trap is made from wire mesh or glass and has two funnel entrances or openings. Here you also put bread crumbs inside the trap and lower it to the bottom. Wait a few hours or leave it in the water overnight; minnows that go inside to feed will become trapped.

Minnow bucket

After you catch the minnows you can keep them alive in a big cagelike box made from wire mesh. This is lowered into the water where the minnows will live for many days. When you go fishing, keep the minnows in a minnow bucket such as the one shown in the drawing. Or get one of those Styrofoam coolers used for picnics and keep the minnows with water inside of it. Don't try to keep minnows in an ordinary can or pail; the water will get warm, and the minnows will die.

For best results you should use live minnows on the hook. As soon as a minnow dies, take it off the hook and replace it with a live one. You can hook a minnow through the back or through both lips. Small minnows from 1½ to 2 inches long are best for panfish such as crappies, white bass, and yellow perch; for trout, minnows from 2 to 3 inches long are best; while for bass you can use minnows from 3 to 5 or 6 inches long. For

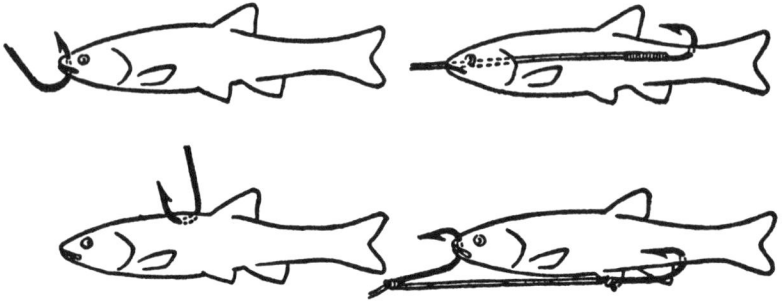

**Hooking minnows**

big fish such as pike, muskellunge, or lake trout, minnows or other small fish up to 10 or 12 inches long are
sometimes used.

## Grasshoppers and Crickets

There are many kinds of grasshoppers that can be
used as bait in freshwater fishing. They are found in
fields, in gardens, and in the grass and weeds along
country roads. You can catch grasshoppers with your
hands or by using a small butterfly net. The best time
to catch grasshoppers is early in the morning, when
the grass is still wet, before the sun gets too high.

Crickets can also be caught in many of the same
places where grasshoppers are found. In addition, they
can be found by turning over flat stones, leaves, hay,
or any other objects found in the fields.

You can keep both grasshoppers and crickets in a
box or other container filled with grass or leaves. The

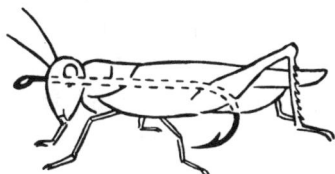

grasshopper

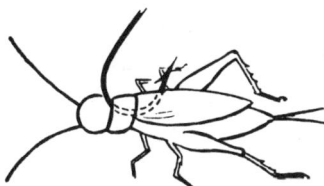

cricket

Hooking grasshopper and cricket

container should have some kind of small opening with a cover through which you can remove the insects. For hooking a grasshopper or cricket (see illustration), use a small, fine wire hook. These two insects can be used for trout, bass, and panfish.

## Hellgrammites

The hellgrammite is a water insect that in its adult stage becomes a dobsonfly. It is dark brown or black, with two sharp pincers, or nippers, and many legs. It grows to be about 3 inches long and lives in many freshwater streams and rivers. Hellgrammites are found under rocks in the riffles, or fast-flowing, shallow waters. All you have to do to catch them is hold a wire or cloth screen on a wooden frame a few feet downstream from the flat rocks. Then you turn over the rocks and the current will wash the hellgrammites onto the wire screen. You can then remove the hellgrammites from the screen and drop them into a small box or can filled with wet leaves. If you let it, a hellgrammite will bite you with the pincers on its head, but if you grab it by the collar behind its head it can't bite. When you use a hellgrammite, run the hook under its hard collar, as shown in the illustration. It will stay alive a long time on the hook this way. Hellgrammites make a good bait for smallmouth black bass, trout, and panfish.

## Crayfish

Crayfish, or crawfish, look like small lobsters and are found in brooks, streams, rivers, and lakes. During the day they hide under stones, around weeds, or in holes in the mud. You can catch them by turning over stones

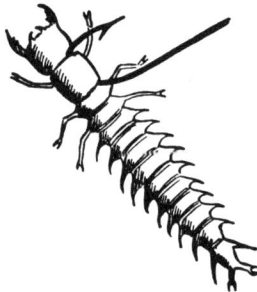

Hooking hellgrammite

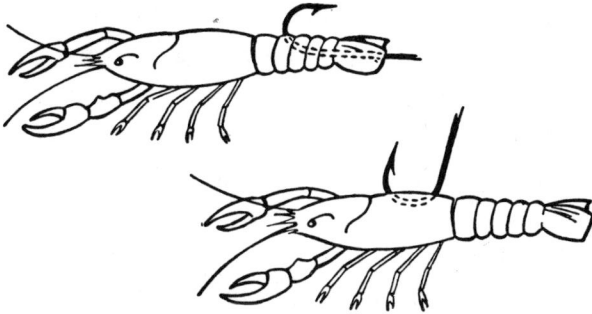

Hooking crayfish

or poking with a stick in the weeds. Grab them by the back so that they won't be able to bite you with their claws. At night the crayfish come out of their hiding places and are easier to catch, with the help of a flashlight.

After you catch the crayfish you can keep them in a box filled with damp moss or leaves. Crayfish are hooked either through the tail or the back. If you catch a soft crayfish that has just shed its hard shell, this makes the best bait of all. But it is hard to keep on the hook unless you tie it on with rubber bands or sewing thread. If you use a hard crayfish it's a good idea to break off the two big claws. Crayfish will catch bass, trout, walleyes, catfish, and other freshwater fish.

## Frogs

Many kinds of small frogs can be used for bait. Green frogs, leopard frogs, pickerel frogs, and small bullfrogs are all good. They are found in the water or on land along the shores of brooks, streams, and lakes. You can catch them by hand or with a small dip net. Keep them in a small wooden box or can filled with damp leaves or grass until you are ready to use them. The best way to hook a frog is through both lips. If you don't like to do this, you can also use a special "frog harness," which can be bought in a fishing tackle store.

When using frogs, let them swim around freely on top or under the water. If a fish grabs the frog give him plenty of time to swallow it. Then strike with your rod —jerk it upward quickly—and set the hook. Frogs will catch bass, big trout, pickerel, pike, and catfish.

## Other Baits

There are many other baits you can use when fresh-water fishing. In fact, almost any small worm, insect,

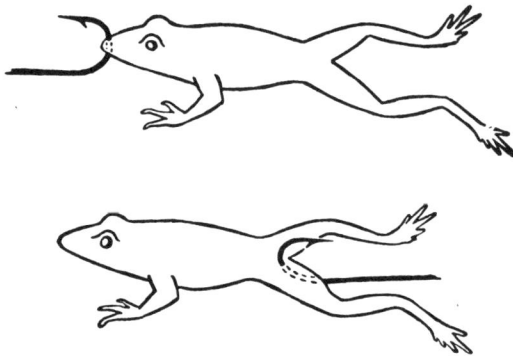

Hooking frogs

or creature that flies, hops, or crawls can be tried for bait. Many kinds of caterpillars make good bait. So do grubs and other small worms found in the ground or in rotten logs. All kinds of beetles and bugs are also eaten by fish. Small lizards or salamanders, which are found in streams or on land, can be used for bait. In the water you'll find small crawling nymphs and larvae that can be put on a hook.

The important thing to remember about using bait is that it should be alive at all times. If the bait dies, take it off the hook and replace it with a live one. And keep your bait moving at regular intervals to attract fish. Bait that doesn't move or hides under a rock or in the weeds won't catch many fish.

Another thing to remember about natural baits is that different states and localities have different laws about catching and using them. Find out from your fishing bureau or fish and game department if the bait you plan to use is legal in your waters.

# 6. Freshwater Lures

Most anglers agree that using artificial lures is one of the most exciting ways to catch fish. It is also less trouble and cleaner than fishing with natural, or live, baits. Many anglers dislike handling or killing live baits such as worms, insects, or frogs, and so prefer to use the artificial lures.

The drawback is that there are thousands of artificial lures on the market. When you walk into a fishing tackle store, you see so many different lures in various sizes, weights, shapes, and colors that you get confused. Before you can decide which to buy, you must learn something about the different lures. Then you can choose a good assortment to use.

Fishing lures are usually designed to look like something fish eat. They represent small flies or other insects, minnows or other fish, crayfish, frogs, or small animals. Of course, not all lures look like something to eat. Some of them look strange—like nothing on this earth. Yet they often catch more fish than lures that resemble something alive. That is because fish strike lures for many reasons. Most of the time they grab a lure because they are hungry. But there are times when they strike a lure because they are curious or angry, or because it invades their territory or spawning bed. Fish can also be very fussy; one day they will take one kind of lure and on the following day they will want another kind. So it pays to carry a good assortment of fishing lures on each trip.

Fishing lures fall into many classes such as flies, bass bugs, spoons, spinners, plugs, jigs, and plastic worms or lures. There are also combinations of all these lures. We will take them up one by one so that you can become familiar with the best lures to buy and use.

## Flies

Artificial flies are made from feathers, hair, fur, wool, tinsel, plastics, and other fuzzy and fish-attracting materials. These are tied around a hook to look like flies and various insects found above and below the water. We usually divide flies into four classes: dry flies, wet flies, nymphs, and streamer or bucktail flies.

A dry fly is made to float on top of the water. Dry flies have stiff, bulky hackles and long tails that support them on the surface, and are tied on thin, light-wire hooks to help them float. Anglers often apply waterproof fly dressing to keep the fly floating longer. You can buy fly dressing in any fishing tackle store.

There are many different kinds of dry flies. The most common dry fly is called a divided-wing fly and has two erect, separate wings. Other dry flies—the fan wing, spent wing, hackle, variant, spider, and bivisible—vary somewhat in construction.

Dry flies come tied on different sizes of hooks, usually from No. 8 to No. 20 or 22. The No. 8 is the larger size and the No. 22 is the smallest. Sizes 10 to 16 are usually used for most trout fishing.

Of the thousands of different patterns of dry flies, the following is a good beginners' assortment: Adams, Blue Dunn, Black Gnat, Brown Bi-visible, Badger Bi-visible, Light Cahill, Quill Gordon, Hendrickson, Gray Wulff, Brown Spider, and Royal Coachman. These dry flies are good in many parts of the country, but if a good fisherman or the tackle dealer recommends others, include them in your tackle kit too.

Wet flies are made to sink below the surface of the water. Each represents an insect that is drowned or struggling under the water. Wet flies are tied on heavy-wire hooks to make them sink faster, and are less bulky than dry flies—a minimum of hair or feathers is used when making them. The standard wet fly has one or two wings, curved low over the body. There are other kinds of wet flies, such as the hackle wet fly, which is sparsely tied and has no wings, and the hair wing, which has wings made of animal hair instead of feathers. Another, the palmer hackle wet fly, has hackle wound around the whole length of the body and resembles a hairy caterpillar.

Most wet flies are tied on hooks from No. 4, the largest, to No. 18, the smallest. The larger sizes are often used when fishing for black bass or big trout. Trout anglers usually get wet flies in sizes Nos. 8, 10, 12, 14, and 16. There are also wet flies made to catch Atlantic salmon, which are larger than those used to catch trout. As with dry flies, there are thousands of different kinds, but the following is a good assortment to start with: the Dark Cahill, Blue Dunn, Gold-Rib Hare's Ear, Gray Hackle, Quill Gordon, Campbell's Fancy, Parmachene Belle, Royal Coachman, and the Wooly Worm.

Nymphs are similar to wet flies in that they are also fished underwater. They differ in appearance, however, since they usually represent the larvae of various aquatic insects. These insects spend part of their lives underwater before they hatch, rise to the surface, and fly away. While the insect is living in the water, it is

dry fly

wet fly

nymph

streamer

bucktail

Flies

called a nymph. Nymphs are also tied on heavy-wire hooks and are made from various materials such as feathers, hair, fur, wool, yarn, floss, rubber, plastic, wire, and lead. Most nymphs are drab in color—brown, gray, or black, with light cream or yellow bellies—and imitate such natural nymphs as the mayfly, stone fly, and caddis larva.

The other flies used for trout and bass fishing are the

streamers and bucktails. Although they are called flies, streamers and bucktails actually look like small minnows or tiny fish. They are long and are tied on long-shanked hooks. The name streamer is applied to those that have long feather wings. The name bucktail is used for those that have wings of hair, usually from the tail of a deer. The bodies of both types are generally silver or gold tinsel. Some of the most popular patterns of streamers and bucktails are the Gray Ghost, Black Ghost, Green Ghost, Mickey Finn, Supervisor, Edson Tiger, and Dark Tiger. Get these in two or three different sizes, such as Nos. 4, 6, and 8. The Marabou streamers in different colors are also very good.

Flies are used with fly-fishing tackle for trout, bass, pickerel, and panfish. Some flies are also used in combination with spinners. When you buy flies you should get the more expensive, well-tied flies. Cheap flies are often useless, since they fall apart, do not float well, and, worst of all, do not catch many fish.

## Bass Bugs

Bass bugs are similar to flies except that they are usually larger and more bulky, resembling big bugs, bettles, moths, and butterflies. Some are also made to resemble minnows, small fish, and frogs. Bass bugs are fished on the surface of the water with a fly rod and have bodies made from cork, wood, plastic, or hair, with wings and tails of feathers or hair. You should get

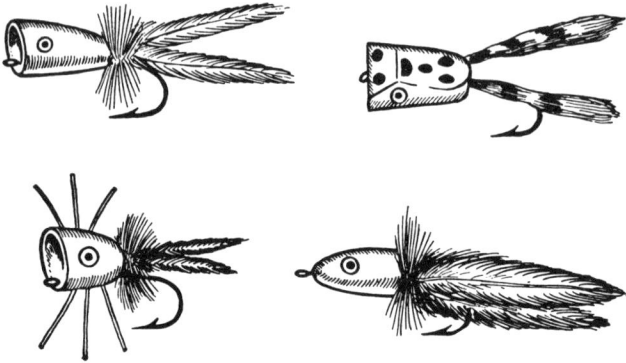

Bass bugs

bass bugs in various sizes and types. The large ones are best for bass. The smaller ones can be used for trout and panfish.

## Spoons

Spoons are among the oldest fishing lures used by human beings. Spoons made from seashells and bone were used as far back as 3000 B.C. Today most of these lures are made from brass, copper, or stainless steel. Some of them are nickel-plated or chrome-plated to make them silvery. Others are painted in different colors.

Spoons are so called because they often resemble a tablespoon with the handle cut off. However, there are many other sizes, shapes, and weights. Some are short, others long and narrow; some oval, others shaped like small fish. Most of them are bent into a concave or

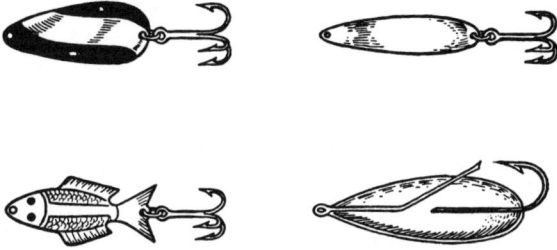

Spoons

curved shape so that they wobble back and forth in the water. Spoons come with single, double, or treble hooks. The majority have a treble hook attached to the tail end.

You can obtain spoons in different sizes and weights for almost any kind of fishing. There are tiny spoons suitable for use with a fly rod. Spoons of 1½ or 2 inches are best for spinning tackle; larger spoons up to 3 or 4 inches are used with bait-casting tackle, while the biggest sizes, up to 5 or 6 inches long, are used when trolling for large fish such as lake trout, pike, and muskellunge.

## Spinners

Spinners are somewhat similar to spoons, but they have thin blades that revolve around a wire shaft. These blades come in different shapes, such as the oval, egg, willow leaf, and kidney. Another popular shape is called the Indiana. Spinners usually have one or two blades, but spinners with three or more blades are used for some types of fishing. Some spinners are weighted for casting, while others are used only for trolling. Spinners can have a single hook or a treble hook attached. You can use those with a bare hook by adding a natural bait such as a worm or minnow. Other spinners have flies, hair, feathers, plastic lures, or pork rind on the hook. Spinners come in various sizes, according to the length and width of the blade. Sizes No. 0 and No. 1 are the smallest, while size No. 7 is one of the largest. You should have an assortment of various kinds and sizes of spinners in your tackle box for different kinds of fishing.

## Spinnerbaits

In recent years a new type of spinner has made an appearance and has proven to catch a lot of bass. Called a spinnerbait, it has two wire arms with one or two spinners on the top arm and a weighted hook on

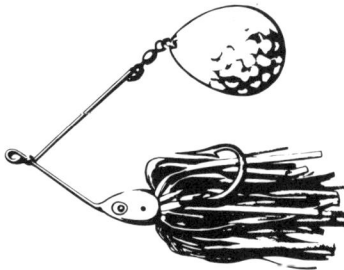

Spinnerbait

the other or lower arm. The hook is usually covered with a plastic skirt or a worm or hair.

## Plugs

Plugs are lures made from wood or plastic to imitate small minnows, fish, frogs, crayfish, bugs, or other small creatures. There are many different types and shapes on the market in every color and design. You can simplify things by dividing plugs into two classes: surface plugs and underwater plugs.

The surface plugs, also called top-water plugs, float at rest and travel on top when you reel them in. Most of them cause some kind of commotion or splash on top of the water to imitate a crippled fish or other small creature. They have cupped heads, metal lips, propellers, or other devices for creating a splash or ripple.

The underwater plugs can be subdivided into two classes: those that float on top of the water and then dive when they are reeled in, and those that sink slowly as soon as they hit the water. Most underwater plugs have angled or grooved heads or metal or plastic lips that cause them to dive and wriggle like small fish. Some of the newer plugs, called crankbaits, dive many feet below the surface when reeled or trolled at a fast speed. Other swimming-type plugs made of balsa wood or light plastic imitate natural minnows in color and action and catch a lot of fish.

Plugs come in different colors, but the most popular finish is the natural fish scale with silver or gold sides.

Others are red, white, or darker colors with designs to imitate frogs or crayfish. Plugs come in different sizes and weights for all types of fishing. Those weighing from ¼ to ½ ounce are best for light spinning tackle. Plugs from ½ to 1 ounce are used with bait-casting tackle or heavy spinning rods or when trolling for big fish such as big bass, pike, muskellunge, lake trout, or salmon. It's a good idea to carry a wide assortment of plugs in your tackle box. (The illustration shows the most popular types of plugs.)

## Plastic Worms and Lures

Plastic worms have become one of the best lures to use in fresh water for bass. They look like big night

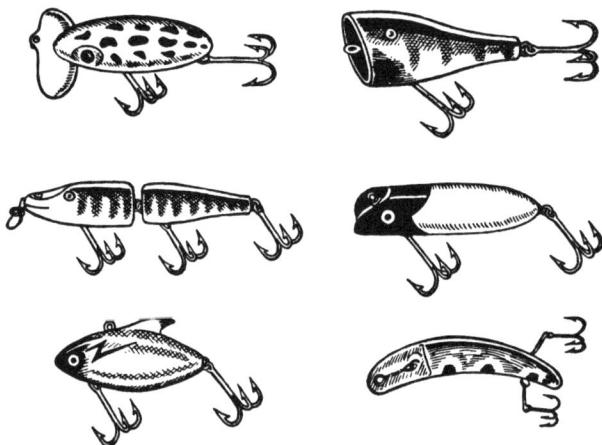

Freshwater plugs

crawlers but come in various colors and lengths. The most popular plastic worms are those that are 6 or 8 inches long, but some are made as long as 12 or even 14 inches to catch big bass. Black, purple, and blue worms are used by most anglers, but other colors such as red, green, yellow, white, or natural worm colors also catch fish. Other plastic lures are made to imitate lizards, frogs, minnows, or crayfish.

## Jigs

When jigs first came out they were used to catch saltwater fish, but in recent years these lures have been used very successfully for freshwater fish such as bass, walleyes, freshwater striped bass, pike, big

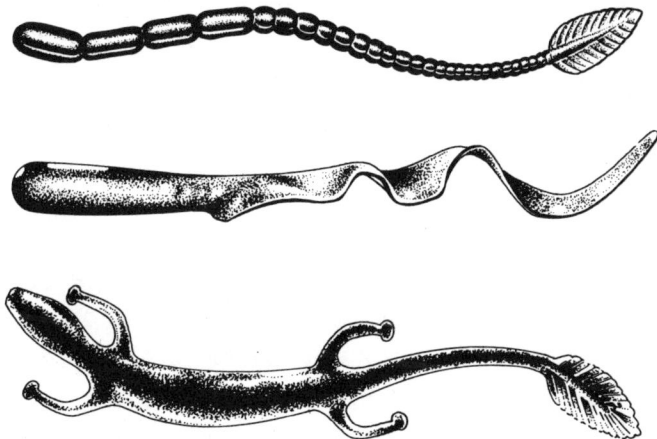

Plastic worms and lizard

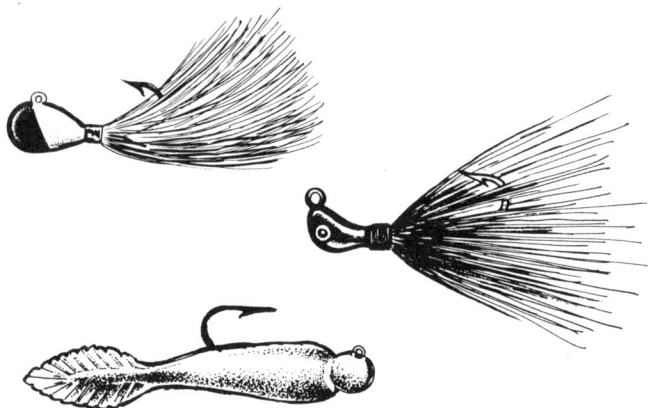

Freshwater jigs

trout, and even catfish. A jig is a simple lure consisting of a lead head molded around a hook. The hook is usually dressed with feathers, hair, or a plastic worm or grub. Jigs also come in various colors and weights, with those running from ⅛ ounce to 1 ounce the most popular sizes.

## Pork Rind

Pork rind—the thick, tough skin from a pig—can be used alone or together with other lures to catch fish. It can be bought in jars in any fishing tackle store. The pork rind comes in strips of varying lengths, widths, and shapes. You can put a strip of pork rind on a plain hook and catch fish such as pickerel by skipping or "skittering" it along the surface of the water with a cane pole. Strips of pork rind can also be added to the hooks of spoons, spinners, and jigs.

Pork chunks also can be used as lures. Here you use the skin as well as some of the fat, cut in the shape of a frog or in a chunk. These are cast around lily pads and worked on the surface for black bass. Pork chunks can also be bought in jars in any fishing tackle store.

Still another pork lure is the black eel strip, which is long, narrow, and dyed black to look like a small eel. They come in two sizes, for spinning or bait-casting tackle. A hook is usually attached at the head of this eel pork strip, which is fished deep, near the bottom.

pork rind

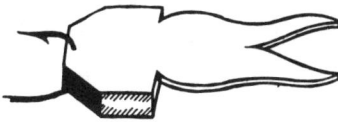

pork chunk

pork eel

Pork lures

The pork eel can also be added to a black lead jig head, which provides casting weight and also sinks the lure deeper in a shorter time. These pork eels come prepared ready for use in jars and are sold by most fishing tackle stores.

Pork rind is preserved in a special liquid and should always be put back into the jar immediately following use, since it dries out when exposed to air and heat. It also weakens with age, and a single strip of pork rind should not be used more than twice.

# 7. Making Freshwater Lures

Most of the artificial lures described in the previous chapter can be made at home. You not only save money by making your own fishing lures, but you have a lot of fun. Making fishing lures also gives you something to do during the long winter months when you are less likely to go fishing. You can make up enough lures during the winter months to last you throughout the fishing season.

## Tying Flies

To tie your own flies for trout or bass fishing, you need a few simple tools that can be bought in many fishing tackle stores: a fly-tying vise, which is specially made for holding hooks when you are tying flies; one or two pairs of fine scissors, with sharp points made for flytiers; hackle pliers, which are used to hold the tip of a feather when winding it around the hook; a dubbing needle (this can be bought cheaply, or you can make your own—get a large sewing needle and push the eye end into a cork bottle stopper); fly-tying thread in sizes oo, ooo, and oooo; clear fly-tying cement or clear lacquer.

Of course, you also need many kinds of fly-tying materials, such as floss, chenille, wool, tinsel, bucktail, squirrel tail, hackle feathers, wing feathers, peacock herl, and peacock sword. And to complete the list you need an assortment of hooks of various sizes in Model Perfect, Sproat, Limerick, and Humpback patterns.

Instead of buying all these fly-tying tools and materials separately, you can simplify matters by buying a complete fly-tying kit. Such a kit will include all the necessary tools and materials for tying all kinds of flies, and is carried by most fishing tackle stores. Or you can order one by mail from one of the companies listed at the end of this chapter.

## Tying a Bucktail

One of the easiest flies to tie is a bucktail. Place a Limerick or other long-shanked hook in the vise. Then take your fine tying thread and tie it onto the shank of the hook about ⅛ of an inch behind the eye of the hook.

Then tie on the end of the flat tinsel with three extra turns of thread, and wind the tinsel around the hook shank up to the bend. (See *A*.) The tinsel should be wound closely, so that there are no spaces. Now bind on a tail, perhaps two tips of hackle feather, by winding the tinsel around it. Then wind the tinsel back toward the eye of the hook. When you reach the eye with the tinsel, make one or two turns of thread around the tinsel and then cut off the tinsel. Then make three more turns of thread to cover the end of the tinsel, and bind it off with a half hitch. (See *B*.) Next you take some white bucktail hair and place it on top of the hook shank and wind several turns of thread around it. Then cut off at a slant the ends of the bucktail hair, which are protruding over the eye of the hook, as shown in *C*. Finish the job by winding thread around the head

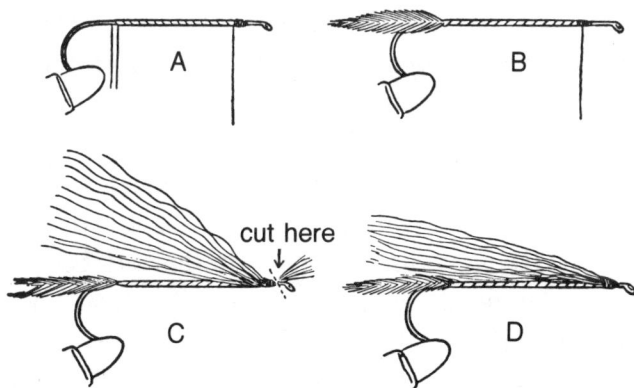

Tying a bucktail fly

(the cut end of the bucktail), tapering toward the eye, and complete the wrapping with a series of half hitches or a whip finish. See *D* for the finished bucktail fly.

The wet fly, dry fly, and nymph are tied in similar fashion, but with variations and different materials. If you can't find anyone to show you how to tie these flies step by step, buy a book on fly tying. There are several such books available.

## Making a Bass Bug

To make a bass bug you need a cork body such as a small cork bottle stopper. This is then shaped with a razor blade and sandpaper (see page 56). Then you slit the cork lengthwise for a depth of about ⅛ of an inch. You can use a small hacksaw to do this. Now get a hump-shanked hook in size 2/0 and wind two or three hackle-feather points near the bend of the hook. After the feathers are wound in place, continue winding the tying silk along the shank of the hook up to the eye. Finish the wrapping with a series of half hitches and cut off the thread.

Now get some plastic resin glue, which comes in powder form at any hardware store. Mix it with water, and apply the glue inside the slit in the cork body and around the shank of the hook. You can use a knife blade to work the glue into the slit in the cork. Then force the hook shank into this slit. Wind some thread tightly around the cork body. Now set the cork aside to allow the glue to dry. In the meantime, get some bucktail hair and tie two wings for the bass bug, cutting the bucktail about 1¼ inches in length for each and winding the ends with thread. Then take the cork body and make two holes, one on each side, about ¼ inch deep, for the bucktail wings. Next force some glue into these holes, applying glue also to the ends of the bucktail wings, and push the wings into the holes. The cork bass bug is now finished except for painting it white, yellow, black, or brown. Use either quick-drying enamel paint or lacquer, and apply it to the cork body, being careful not to get any paint on the feathers or wings.

## Making a Spoon

Spoons can be made very easily if you order the finished bodies and parts from a mail-order house, such as those listed at the end of this chapter. These companies have all sizes of spoons in various shapes, weights, and finishes. You get the metal bodies and also some split rings and treble hooks. These spoon bodies have two holes, one on each end. Take a knife blade and spread one of the split rings, forcing it into the hole on

split ring

split ring       spoon       treble hook       spoon assembled

Assembling a spoon

the tail end of the spoon. Then force the treble hook into the ring. The other split ring is spread and forced through the other end of the spoon, and then attached to the line. (See illustration.)

## Making a Spinner

The parts needed to make a spinner can also be obtained from a mail-order supply house. To make a complete spinner you will need blades, beads, clevises, stainless-steel wire, and hooks. The most popular spinner blade is the Indiana type, in nickel-plated finish. You can get this blade and other types in different sizes to make spinners for all your fishing needs.

To make a simple spinner, cut about an 8-inch length of size No. 10 stainless-steel wire. Then form a locking eye on one end of this wire. To cut the wire use diagonal cutting pliers. To form the locking eye use round-nose pliers. The drawings below show how to form this

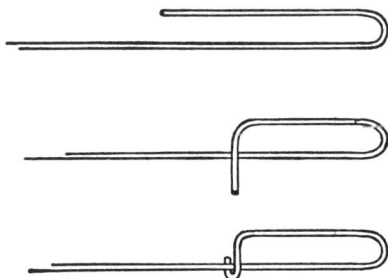

Forming locking eye

eye. After the locking eye is finished get four to six beads and slip them on the wire so that they rest against the locking eye. Then put a spinner blade on the clevis and slide the wire shaft through the two holes of the clevis. To finish the spinner, form another eye on the end of the wire to take the line. The finished spinner will look like the one in the illustration. This type of spinner is best for trolling, but if you add a clincher sinker to the leader or line, it can be cast. You can also make a weighted spinner for casting by using metal beads or weights on the spinner wire.

To use the spinner all you have to do is add a single hook to the locking eye. You can put a worm, strip of pork rind, or a minnow on this hook. Instead of a bare hook you can also add a treble hook with bucktail or feathers, or you can attach a fly to the locking eye.

## Making Plugs

To make plugs for freshwater fishing you need some kind of wood that can be worked easily with hand tools such as a knife, saw, file, and wood drill. Almost any wood can be used to make plugs, but woods such as cedar, birch, and basswood are best since they are

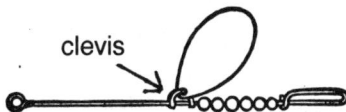

Finished spinner

light, float well, and are easy to carve. Such woods are sold in most lumberyards. You can start with a block of wood and whittle a plug with a sharp knife. Or you can put the block of wood in a vise and use a rasp to form the plug. Then you can use a smooth wood file and sandpaper to finish it off. You can also buy round, wooden dowels and make many plugs with these by just shaping the ends after you cut off a section.

You can save even more work if you order ready-shaped wood or plastic bodies from a mail-order supply house. These plug bodies come finished except for the hardware, which is added to them. To complete a plug, you need screws, screw eyes or hook holders, and treble hooks.

The four basic freshwater plugs you can make easily are shown in the drawing. The first plug shown is the popper type, which can be 3 inches long and 1 inch in diameter at the wide end or head. The tail end tapers to a diameter of $\frac{3}{8}$ inch. The face or front of the plug is carved like a dish or cup so that it will throw water when jerked.

The second plug you can make is the wobbler type, which is about $3\frac{3}{4}$ inches long and $\frac{7}{8}$ inch wide. It tapers to a point at the tail. The head of this plug is cut at an angle and can be grooved.

The next plug is the darter type, which is also $3\frac{3}{4}$ inches long and $\frac{3}{4}$ inch in width. A notch is cut in the head, and the top of the head is filed, as shown in the drawing.

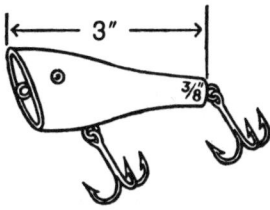

popper

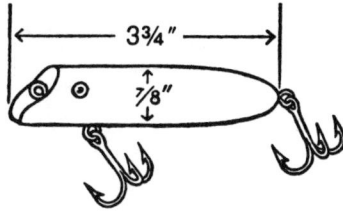

wobbler

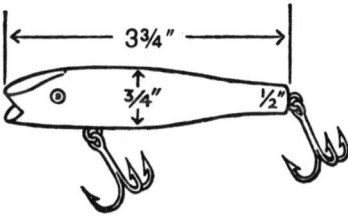

darter

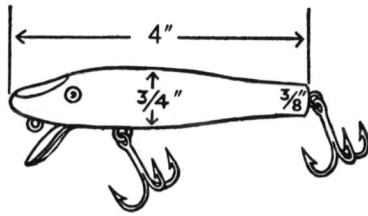

underwater

Plug types

Finally, we have the underwater plug, which is 4 inches in length and ¾ inch wide. This plug tapers toward the tail, where it is ⅜ inch wide. For this plug you will need a metal lip, which is screwed in under the plug near the head. You can cut such a lip from sheet metal of brass, copper, or aluminum. Bend it as shown in the drawing on the next page and give the lip a shape like a shallow cup, using a ball peen hammer. Then drill three holes in the metal lip and screw it on the plug body. Finished, ready-to-use metal lips can be ordered from some mail-order houses.

The sizes above are suggested for bait-casting plugs

bend here

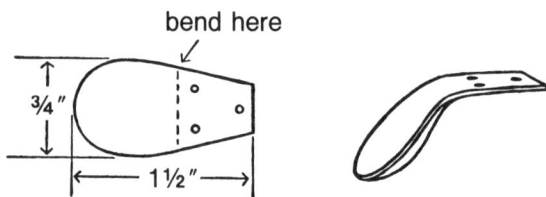

Metal lip

and most spinning tackle. But you can make them smaller and lighter to use with light spinning outfits.

The plugs are assembled by screwing in the treble hooks. A screw eye is opened, and the hook eye is slipped into it. Then it is closed, and the screw eye is screwed into the wooden body of the plug. Use an awl or ice pick to make a hole in the wood to get the screw eye started.

After the plugs have been assembled they should be painted with enamel or lacquer. Lacquers dry faster but do not give as smooth a finish as enamels. If you have an airbrush, you can spray lacquers and do a good job. You can also buy a can of pressurized spray paint and spray the plugs white or silver. No matter what color or colors you paint the plug finally, you should give it at least two coats of white paint or lacquer first to waterproof the wood. Then you can add any other colors you want.

The following mail-order companies sell parts and materials for tying flies and making fishing lures.

Write them for their catalogs:

Herter's Inc., RFD 2, Interstate 90, Mitchell, S.Dak. 57301

Limit Manufacturing Corp., Box 369, Richardson, Tex. 75080

Netcraft Co., Box 5510, Toledo, Ohio 43613

Reed Tackle, Box 390, Caldwell, N.J. 07006

# 8. Freshwater Fish

## Trout

The trout family are among the most popular fish caught in fresh water. These fish, which are found mostly in cold-water streams, rivers, and lakes, are all noted as great fighters on the end of a line. Trout are also highly prized because they make particularly good eating.

There are many different kinds of trout found in the United States and Canada. The most popular varieties are described here.

Brook trout

The brook trout is often called the native trout because it was the only trout found in the northeastern part of the United States when the first white settlers arrived. Later, brook trout were introduced in the West, and today they are found mostly in the northern part of the United States and Canada. They are also called mountain trout, brookie, speckled trout, and squaretail.

Brook trout like clean, cold water and are most numerous in the smaller, spring-fed streams in mountain and wilderness areas. They often live in tiny feeder streams that are so narrow you can step or jump across them. But in Canada and other northern areas, they are often found in large rivers and lakes.

The average brook trout is on the small side when caught, weighing from ½ to 1 pound. However, in some of the larger rivers and lakes, they may reach a much bigger size. The world's record brook trout caught on rod and reel was caught in the Nipigon River in Ontario, Canada, and weighed 14½ pounds.

The brook trout is a beautiful, brightly colored fish, with a speckled back and sides, red spots, and pink fins edged with white.

The rainbow trout is another handsome, hard-fighting favorite with fly-fishermen. It grows larger than the brook trout and is most common in the West, where it is native; but rainbow trout have also been introduced into many other waters of the northern United States. Some rainbow trout also thrive in our southern states in the colder rivers and lakes.

You can usually identify rainbow trout by the black spots all over the body and fins, and also by the pink or purplish-red band that runs along the sides of the fish from the head to the tail.

Rainbow trout are found mostly in the faster-flowing portions of the larger streams, rivers, and lakes. They like to migrate or travel, swimming up and down rivers and streams and entering lakes or the ocean. Some rainbows near the Pacific Coast migrate to the sea and are then called steelhead. After living in the sea for a while, they change color and become steel blue and

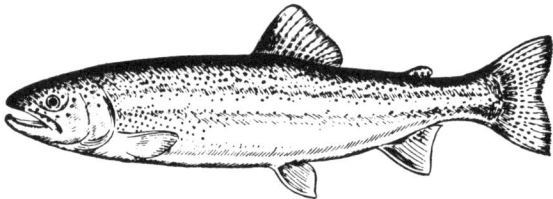

Rainbow trout

silvery in appearance. The spots and pink band fade and become less noticeable.

The size of the rainbow caught will depend on the waters where it is found. In most small streams they run from about 1 pound to 5 pounds in weight. In the larger rivers and lakes they reach a much bigger size. The largest caught on rod and reel weighed 42 pounds.

Now we come to the brown trout, which has rapidly taken over many waters in this country. At one time there were no brown trout in the United States. Then some brown-trout eggs were imported from Europe, and the young trout were planted in waters all over the United States. Today they are numerous in most of our northern states, some southern states, and parts of Canada.

The brown trout can stand warmer waters than either the brook or rainbow trout. It is also a harder fish to catch and can survive in streams that are heavily fished. Because of this you will find that most of the trout found in streams near our larger cities are the smart brown trout.

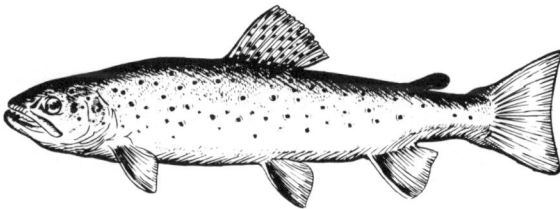

Brown trout

Brown trout are so called because they are dark brown on the back, blending into a lighter brown on the sides. They also have some black, brown, and red spots on the back and sides.

The brown trout reaches a big size in the larger rivers and lakes, where the biggest caught on rod and reel weighed over 30 pounds. However, in most streams and lakes brown trout will run from about 1 pound to 8 or 10 pounds in weight.

Some of the other trout caught include the cutthroat, Dolly Varden, and golden trout. The cutthroat trout gets its name from the red streak on both sides of the lower jaw. It is found from California to Alaska along our Pacific coast and also in the Rocky Mountains. Cutthroat trout usually weigh from 1 to 6 pounds, but the world's record is 41 pounds.

The Dolly Varden trout is another that is common in western waters, where it is found from California to Alaska. It has red and orange spots on the body, and the lower fins are edged with white, like those of the brook trout. It can grow to 29 pounds in weight, but in small streams and rivers it usually runs from ½ to 5 pounds.

The golden trout is the most beautiful trout of all, with its golden-yellow sides and its bright red stripe running midway along its body from head to tail. Over this there are dark blotches spaced at regular intervals, usually numbering about ten. This trout is found in only a few places in the West, such as the Sierras of

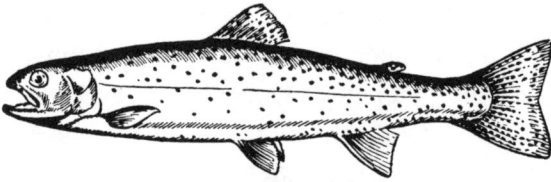

Cutthroat trout

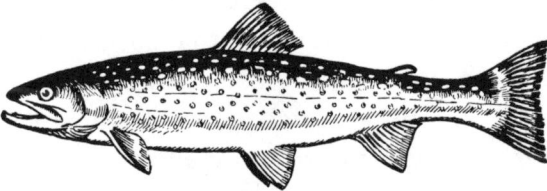

Dolly Varden trout

Golden trout

California. It rarely reaches more than a pound in weight in the smaller streams. The largest golden trout caught on rod and reel weighed 11 pounds.

In general, you will find the best trout fishing in the spring and early summer. The months of May and June are usually good. However, if the water isn't too low or warm, you can often have good fishing during the summer months as well. Fall fishing can also be good, but most trout seasons end by September or October. During the summer months the trout fishing is best early in the morning, in the evening, and at night.

The most difficult part of trout fishing is locating the fish in a stream or lake. Most beginners who go trout fishing concentrate their fishing on the larger pools because of the deeper water. They feel that such spots have more fish. While it is true that pools often contain many trout, these fish are usually resting and are therefore difficult to catch. When trout are actively feeding they will come into shallow and fast water provided there are places such as deep holes, rocks, ledges, and logs where they can lie hidden and protected from the full force of the current. Early in the morning and in the evening, trout will often be found at the tail end of pools and in the shallow fast water. Trout usually face upstream and watch for food being swept their way by the current.

When you fish for trout always approach the water carefully. Avoid casting shadows over water, walk lightly along the bank, and avoid bumping rocks or making waves when wading in the water. You may even have to hide behind a bush if the water is shallow and clear. In small streams it is best to stay out of the water, since any disturbance will frighten the trout. If you do frighten the trout, give the spot a rest for at least half an hour before you fish it again. Fish slowly and don't be afraid to make several casts in a spot that looks good.

In lakes, trout often stay close to shore, where they

can be caught around rocks, logs, overhanging trees, and weeds. They also gather at spots where brooks, streams, or rivers enter the lake. In the summer months trout stay deep and near underwater springs.

When using dry flies for trout in a stream, wade upstream, casting the fly into likely looking spots at an angle above the water you want to cover. Then let the current take the fly downstream as naturally as possible. If the fly starts to drag unnaturally, lift it from the water and make a new cast. Dry flies are best when there are many insects hatching or flying over the water and you see trout feeding on them. But you can also catch trout by casting blindly and hoping that a fish will see the fly and come up for it.

When using wet flies, cast the sinking fly slightly upstream, a few feet above the spot you want to fish. Then let the fly sink and float downstream into the best spots. In the beginning you can let the fly drift naturally in the current; then when it reaches the end of the drift, you can retrieve the wet fly in short jerks.

Nymphs are used somewhat like wet flies in that they are cast up or across the stream and are allowed to sink and drift with the current. Then, when the nymph completes its drift and the line starts to straighten out, you can retrieve it upstream in short jerks. It is important to watch the leader and line carefully for any indication of a strike when fishing with nymphs or wet flies. Sometimes you will see the trout flash under the water as it grabs the lure. Then you should strike immediately to set the hook.

When you use bucktails or streamers, you can cast them across stream or downstream. Then retrieve the fly rapidly in short jerks to imitate a frightened or crippled minnow or other small fish.

In large streams and rivers you can also use a spinning outfit or a bait-casting outfit to catch trout. Then you cast lures such as spoons, spinners, and small plugs, retrieving them by reeling in at various speeds.

Trout can also be caught on natural baits such as worms, minnows, grasshoppers, or other insects. A fly rod can be used with these, since you can cast these baits better and control them in the water. Worms and minnows are especially good baits to use early in the year when the trout season opens and the trout are feeding deep below the surface. Live insects are better later on, during the late spring and summer when they are plentiful and are naturally eaten by trout. When using natural baits it is important to keep them moving. Let the worms and minnows drift naturally with the current, as if they had no line attached. You don't have to strike immediately when a trout takes a natural bait. Instead, give him time to swallow it before you try to set the hook.

## Coho and Chinook Salmon

These two salmon were originally found in salt water and Pacific coastal rivers, but have been introduced into Lake Michigan and the other Great Lakes as well as other fresh waters. They grow big, with the

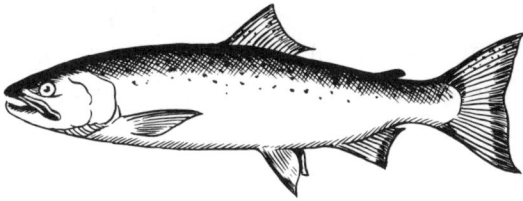

Coho salmon

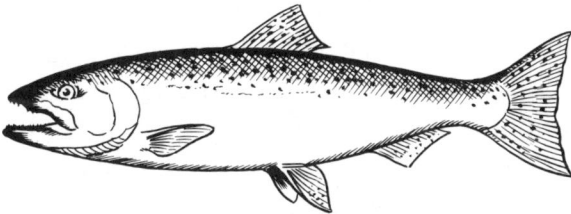

Chinook salmon

coho salmon reaching 30 pounds and the chinook salmon growing up to 100 pounds or more.

During the spring months these salmon move closer to shore and can be caught in the surf, from piers, docks, and small boats. Later on toward the summer months, the salmon go into deeper water. Then in the fall they move back to the shallow water near shore at the mouths of streams and rivers, which they soon enter for spawning purposes.

Both these salmon can be caught by casting from shore with spoons or plugs in the spring. In the fall they can be caught in the rivers by casting spinners, spoons, and flies. But most of the salmon are caught by trolling with spoons, spinners, plugs, and natural baits such as alewives and smelt. In the spring and fall you can troll in shallow water near shore. But during the summer months you have to troll deep using weights, planers, wire lines, or downriggers. Then you have to troll anywhere from 50 to 200 feet deep to catch the salmon.

## Black Bass

The black bass is the favorite freshwater game fish in the United States. More anglers like to fish for bass than any other true game fish. They are more plentiful and found in more areas than trout: almost every large lake or river contains black bass. Most of the freshwater fishing tackle, such as spinning and bait-casting rods and reels, is designed to catch bass. And hundreds if not thousands of lures, such as spinners, spinnerbaits, spoons, plugs, jigs, plastic worms and lures have been made especially for black-bass fishing.

The popularity of the black bass is well deserved since they are a true game fish in every way. They put up a stubborn fight on the end of the line, often leaping out of the water or standing on their tails to shake their heads. Black bass are smart fish and soon learn to avoid lures and baits that are carelessly presented, but will strike well-presented artificial lures regularly. In almost every lake you'll find big, wise black bass that are hard to hook. This makes black-bass fishing a challenge, and if you can catch these fish with some regularity, you can consider yourself a good angler.

There are several species and subspecies of black bass found in the United States. But anglers are most familiar with the largemouth bass and the smallmouth bass. The largemouth bass is also called the bigmouth bass, grass bass, green bass, straw bass, bayou bass, slough bass, lake bass, marsh bass, and linesides. It is pale green along the sides of the body, with a dark-green back and a black stripe running along the sides in the center, starting from the head and ending at the tail. Although this black line is sometimes faint, it is usually quite distinct and can be seen on a fish in the water many feet away. Finally, the largemouth bass has an upper jaw that extends beyond its eye, from which it gets its name.

Largemouth bass are found in almost every state in the country and in parts of Canada. They prefer the warmer lakes, slower rivers, ponds, and other waters where lily pads, weeds, and other vegetation are plentiful.

Most of the largemouth bass caught weigh from 1 to

Largemouth bass

5 pounds. In southern waters, such as the Florida lakes and some lakes in California, bass often reach 10 pounds or more. The largest one ever caught came from Montgomery Lake in Georgia and weighed 22 pounds, 4 ounces.

The smallmouth bass is more bronze or brassy green in color. It has brown or bronze vertical lines on the sides, running from the back to the belly. The jaw of the smallmouth bass doesn't extend beyond its eye when the mouth is closed.

Smallmouth bass are found in many of the same areas as the largemouth and are most plentiful in northern states and in Canada. They are also found in a few of our southern states where the waters are cold. Smallmouth bass are usually found in colder, faster, and cleaner water than the largemouth bass, especially lakes with sand, gravel, or rock bottoms, or streams with fast currents.

Smallmouth bass do not reach as large a size as the

Smallmouth bass

largemouth. The average fish caught runs from 1 to 3 pounds. The largest caught weighed 11 pounds, 15 ounces, and was caught in Dale Hollow Lake, which borders on Kentucky and Tennessee.

Largemouth bass are found in many parts of a lake, depending on the season, the temperature of the water, the type of food present, and the time of day. In the late spring and early summer, when the water warms up, bass move close to shore into shallow water. They stay there to feed and spawn until the water gets too warm. Then they go back into deep water again, especially during the daytime. However, in the evening, at night, and early in the morning, bass often come back to the shallows to feed. So the general rule during the hot, summer months is to fish near shore early in the morning and at night and in deeper water during the daytime.

Largemouth bass in a lake are usually found around lily pads, hyacinths, grass, weeds, and other plants. Sunken trees, logs, and stumps in the water also attract them. In deeper water look for underwater weed beds, drop-offs, submerged points, bars, channels, old riverbeds, and similar bottom structure.

Smallmouth bass in a lake prefer spots with sand, gravel, or rock bottoms. Deep water along rocky shores and cliffs, gravel or rock bars that drop off into deeper water are favorite hangouts for these fish.

Smallmouth bass are also found in rivers and streams. Here they stay in the deeper pools and eddies most of the time, but occasionally they will come into the fast rapids or riffles to feed and can be caught there. They usually stay close to large rocks or boulders in rivers.

One good method of fishing early in the morning or in the evening, when bass are in the shallows, is to row around a lake about 50 feet from shore. Here you usually need two people, one to row the boat and another to cast toward shore. You can use either a spinning or bait-casting rod for this type of fishing. The best lures to use are usually surface plugs such as the poppers, crippled minnows, and floating balsa wood or plastic minnows. Cast the plug as close to shore as possible or else near a stump, log, or lily pads. Then let the plug lie there for about a minute or so. Next you twitch the plug or pop it and let it lie still again. Move or pop it again and let it stay in one place once more. Keep doing this until the plug has almost reached the boat, making the plug imitate a frog or crippled minnow that can't swim too fast.

Some surface plugs have metal lips or wings that create a commotion or fuss on top of the water. These can be reeled steadily at any speed. Try reeling slowly first, then faster on the next cast.

Underwater plugs are also good lures for bass. Some of these float on top of the water, then dive and travel just below the surface. These can be used close to shore, where the water is shallow. But when the bass are in deep water, as is often the case in the middle of the day during the summer, then deep-running underwater plugs or sinking plugs must be used. The so-called crankbaits are plugs that run deep. The closer you get to the bottom with underwater plugs, the better your chances of catching fish.

Plugs that sink are fished close to the bottom simply by letting them go down. When such a plug hits bottom, reel it slowly a few feet, let it pause or sink again, then reel or jerk it again and keep doing this until the plug is near the boat.

Another great lure for largemouth bass is the plastic worm, especially those that are black, purple, or blue in color. These can be rigged with a single hook near the head and fished on top by reeling fast enough to keep the worm on the surface. Or you can let the worm sink to various depths and reel it in slowly with short jerks of the rod. If you are trying to reach bass in deep water, you can add a sliding sinker weight in front of the worm. When fishing in lily pads or weeds or near the bottom in weeds, among sunken trees or brush, the worm should be rigged with a weedless hook or the regular hook can have the point and barb buried inside the worm.

You can also catch bass on spinners and spoons by casting and reeling in at various speeds. For best results try an erratic retrieve with regular sweeps and jerks of the rod tip. Spoons and spinners are especially good lures for smallmouth bass in rivers, since they sink fast in the current and reach the fish deep down.

The lures called spinnerbaits can also be used for bass in heavy weeds by buzzing them (reeling them on top) or by letting them sink down deep.

Bass are often caught by trolling in a lake or river. Here you let the lure out behind the boat and run the outboard motor at a fairly slow speed. The best speed is usually the one that brings the proper action out of a fishing lure. Such lures as underwater plugs, spoons, spinners, and flies or spinners and bait can be used when trolling. In trolling you let out anywhere from 50 to 150 feet of line behind the boat. Usually the more line you let out the deeper the lure will travel.

Another way to catch bass is with a fly rod and flies or bass bugs. Bass bugs are especially good lures when used with a fly rod. You can also use some of the weighted bass bugs with a light spinning rod. When using bass bugs, fish them slowly near shore or in shallow water. Cast out and let the bug lie on top of the water for a minute or more. Then give it a few short jerks or twitches and let it lie still again. Continue doing this until the bug is near you, then cast to another spot and repeat the retrieve.

Bass can also be caught on other fly lures, such as streamers, bucktails, and wet flies. These lures are especially good for smallmouth bass in streams and rivers, which are fished in much the same way as described in the section on trout fishing.

When bass refuse to take artificial lures, they can often be caught on natural baits such as minnows, worms, frogs, hellgrammites, crayfish, and insects.

Minnows can be used in a lake with or without a float or bobber on the line above the hook. If there are a lot of weeds on the bottom, it is better to use a small float, but in open water you can use a minnow alone without the cork or plastic float. Hook the minnow through the lips or back and let it swim around. When you see the float go down or move away, do not pull up immediately but wait a few seconds until the bass has a chance to swallow the small fish. Then, when he starts moving away once more, set the hook. Frogs can be fished the same way—give the bass plenty of time to swallow the bait before striking.

Either the large night crawlers or the small worms, if you put two or three or more on a hook, can be used for bass. Big night crawlers can be used alone, or you can put two of them on a hook. Bass like a lot of worms wriggling, so keep changing the worms if they die. Worms can be fished with a float suspended in the water, or you can use them without the bobber and let them sink slowly. When they reach bottom let them lie there a few minutes. Then bring them in and cast out again. In a stream or river you can also either let the worms drift naturally with the current at various depths or let them go down to the bottom and lie there a while.

Hellgrammites and crayfish can also be fished with or without a float. In lakes it is usually best to use a float, while in streams and rivers it is best to let these baits sink to the bottom or drift with the current.

When fishing for black bass you must use your imagination and experiment with various lures and baits until you find what your fish want. That is why the best fishermen usually carry a great assortment of lures with them on every trip.

# Panfish

The so-called panfish are several small fish that are caught in freshwater lakes and rivers. They include such fish as the sunfish, rock bass, crappies, yellow perch, white perch, and white bass. These small fish are not only good for the pan, or for eating, but also provide good sport with a light fishing outfit such as a fly rod or spinning rod.

SUNFISH

The largest and most popular sunfish is the bluegill. This sunfish is found in many parts of the United States, and it is often stocked in newly built farm ponds. The bluegill is recognized by the black blotch found on the back edge of the gill cover. This sunfish averages from 6 to 8 inches in length and about ½ pound in weight, although from time to time big ones weighing 1, 2, or even 3 pounds are caught. The largest ever caught on rod and reel weighed 4 pounds, 12 ounces.

Another popular sunfish is the pumpkinseed, or common, sunfish. This sunfish doesn't grow as big as the

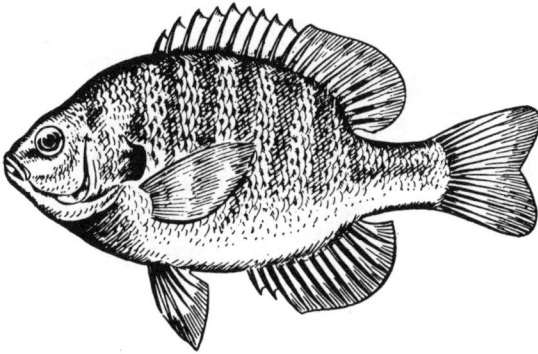

Bluegill sunfish

bluegill, rarely reaching more than 1 pound in weight. Most of them run up to 5 or 6 inches in length. This sunfish is most numerous east of the Mississippi River, but has also been stocked in some western states.

Other sunfish are the green, long-eared, red-breasted, warmouth, and shell-cracker, or red-eared, sunfish. Sunfish are known by many names in various areas and are often called bream in the South. Most sunfish feed on small minnows, worms, grasshoppers, crickets, snails, beetles, and other insects.

ROCK BASS

The rock bass is related to the sunfish and is often called the redeye or goggle-eye. This panfish is bronze or olive green in color and has a red eye.

Rock bass are found mostly in the eastern and midwestern United States. They live in rivers and lakes

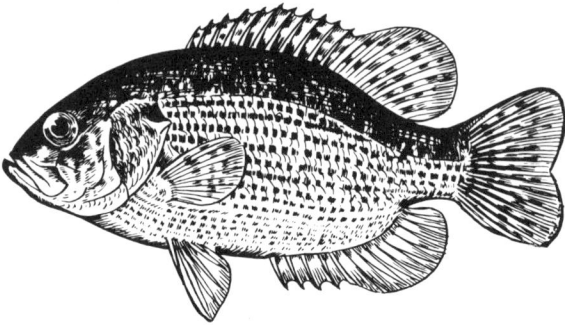

Rock bass

preferring the quieter and deeper parts of streams and rivers.

The average size of the rock bass caught is about ½ pound, but they reach up to 2 pounds.

CRAPPIES

The crappie is another fish that is related to the sunfish, with a similar flat and deep body. There are two kinds of crappies, the white crappie and the black crappie. They look very much alike; the only way to tell the difference is to count the dorsal spines. The white crappie has five to seven spines in the dorsal fin, while the black crappie has seven or more. Both crappies are pale yellow and light green along the back, with irregular spots on their silver sides and belly.

Both species are found in many parts of the country; but the black crappie is most plentiful in the North; the white crappie, in the South. Crappies are called specks

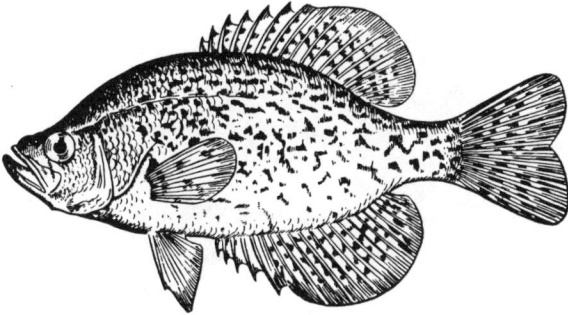

Black crappie

in the South, but they also have many other names.

Most crappies caught weigh ½ to 1 pound, but sometimes they reach as much as 2 or 3 pounds. The largest crappie caught weighed 5¼ pounds. This was a white crappie, which grows larger than the black.

## YELLOW PERCH

The yellow perch is another panfish that is very popular with freshwater anglers. It is easily recognized by its dark olive-green back and stripes over golden yellow sides.

At one time the yellow perch was found only in the eastern part of the United States, from Canada to North Carolina, but it has since been stocked in many other parts of the country.

The yellow perch prefers water somewhat colder and deeper than other panfish like and so is most plentiful in our northern lakes and rivers.

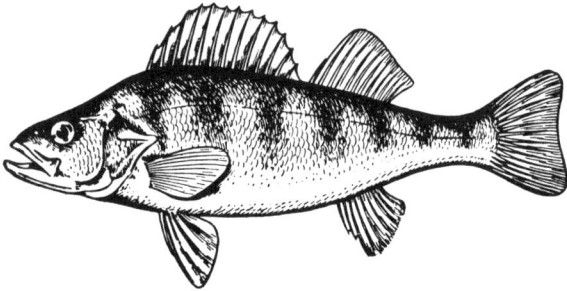

Yellow perch

Most yellow perch run from about 8 to 10 inches in length, depending on the waters in which they are found. In some lakes yellow perch never reach a big size, while in others large perch are common. The largest yellow perch ever caught weighed 4 pounds, 3 ounces.

Yellow perch are considered one of the tastiest panfish in fresh water. For eating purposes, in fact, many anglers prefer yellow perch to bass or even trout.

WHITE PERCH

This panfish is not a true perch but belongs to the sea-bass family. White perch have an olive or dark-green back and silvery sides, and are shaped like the yellow perch. It is a panfish that are caught along the Atlantic coast from Nova Scotia to South Carolina. The white perch can live in salt or brackish water—in fact they prefer rivers that enter the sea. But they can also

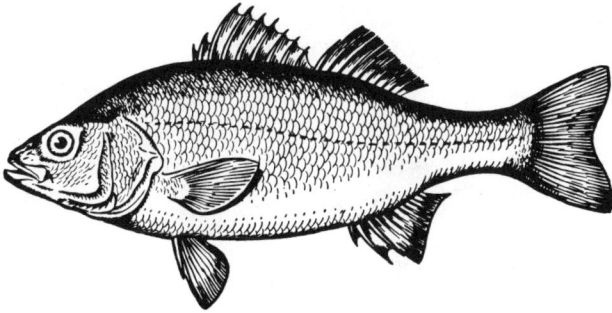

White perch

live in freshwater lakes if trapped or stocked in such waters.

Most white perch average from ½ to 1 pound in weight, although they often reach 2 or 3 pounds. The largest caught on rod and reel weighed 4 pounds, 12 ounces.

WHITE BASS

The white bass resembles the white perch in general appearance. However, the white bass has stripes running along its sides like the striped bass.

These fish are found mostly in the Great Lakes, the Mississippi River and its tributaries, and in the larger lakes and reservoirs of the Middle West and some southern states.

White bass average from 1 to 2 pounds in weight and have been known to reach 4 or 5 pounds.

Almost any freshwater fishing tackle, such as cane

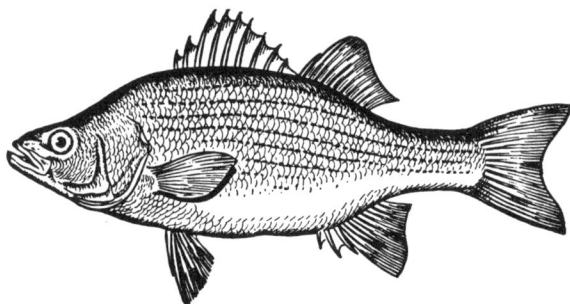

White bass

poles, bait-casting rods, spinning rods, and fly rods, can be used to catch panfish. The most popular is the cane pole with a bobber and live bait, but for the most sport a fly rod is best.

The bait used for most panfish is a small, lively garden worm. Small minnows are good for such fish as crappies, yellow perch, and white bass. Grasshoppers, crickets, beetles, grubs, and mealworms will also catch panfish.

Panfish can also be caught on artificial lures such as small trout flies, tiny streamers, small spoons and spinners, and very small plugs. Small jigs can also be tried near the bottom.

Sunfish and crappies are usually found near shore around weed beds, lily pads, and sunken trees or logs. In rivers they prefer the quieter waters of pools. Yellow perch like deeper water, usually over sunken weeds. White bass are often found in the middle of a lake, chasing smaller bait fish or minnows.

Most panfish travel in schools, and if you catch one you can be pretty sure there are more around. Yellow perch, white bass, and white perch frequently move about from one place to another. To locate them you have to change spots. On some lakes you often see other rowboats anchored and fishing for panfish, or there will be people fishing from piers, docks, or from the shore if panfish are biting. You can fish near them, but not so close as to interfere with their fishing.

Panfish usually bite all day long, but during the hot, summer months the early-morning or late-afternoon hours are best. Yellow perch, white perch, and white bass come close to shore, or head into streams and rivers entering lakes in the spring of the year. Here they lay eggs, or spawn. Fishing is often good during these spring runs if you can find the fish.

In fishing for panfish, a cork or bobber should be used about 4 or 5 feet from the hook. When a fish first takes the bait, let him bite on it until he swallows it and starts moving away. When the float or bobber starts moving fast across the surface or sinks out of sight, lift the pole or rod sharply to set the hook.

If you are using artificial lures such as flies, bugs, spoons, or spinners, do not reel or troll them too fast. Panfish strike a slow-moving lure more readily than a fast-moving lure.

Panfish are usually so plentiful in most waters that you are allowed to keep large catches. In some states and waters there is no limit, and you can keep all you can catch, so be sure that you know your state laws.

It's quite a task cleaning and scaling the smaller panfish; but after that you can look forward to delicious eating when the panfish are fried a golden brown.

## Striped Bass

Most people think of the striped bass as a saltwater fish, but these fish have been caught in freshwater rivers for many years. In recent years they have been stocked in many freshwater lakes, reservoirs, and rivers all over the country, and today you'll find good fishing for the stripers in many states.

You can use the same fishing tackle for striped bass as you do for big bass, pike, or muskies (muskellunge). The striper will also hit many of the same fishing lures, such as spoons, spinners, plugs, and jigs, that are used for these fish. They'll also take small, live eels, shad minnows, herring, and other small fish. You can cut up the larger fish and use the pieces as bait as well.

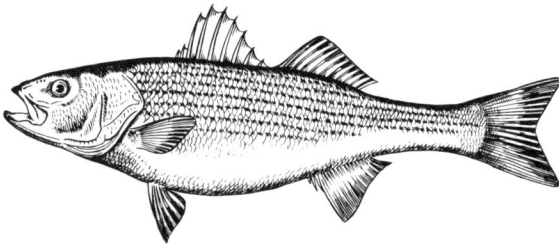

Striped bass

The most exciting fishing for freshwater stripers takes place early in the morning, toward dusk, and sometimes in the middle of the day when they chase the shad minnows or other small fish to the surface. Then you speed over to the spot in your boat where you see birds diving or small fish leaping and cast your lures into the feeding fish.

Stripers are also taken by trolling at various depths with lures. When they are on top chasing small fish, you can troll your lures shallow just below the surface. But when you see no stripers feeding, especially during the middle of the day, you have to troll deep to catch these fish. Then you use weights on your line, wire line, or downriggers to get the lures deep enough.

Freshwater stripers grow big, and many fish weighing from 1 pound or 2 up to 20 or 30 pounds are caught. They reach over 50 or even 60 pounds in weight in some big lakes and reservoirs.

## The Pike Family

The members of the pike family are the muskellunge, the pike, and the pickerel. They all look alike in general body shape, but vary in size and color.

### MUSKELLUNGE

The muskellunge, or muskie, is one of our largest freshwater game fish. It has an olive-green back, gray sides, and dark spots and irregular stripes or bars over

Muskellunge

its body and fins. The muskellunge has a large mouth and jaws resembling an alligator. Most muskellunge run from 10 to 30 pounds in weight. The largest one caught on rod and reel weighed 69 pounds, 15 ounces.

Muskellunge are found in the Saint Lawrence River, Great Lakes Basin, and west through southern Canada to Minnesota, and also from northwestern Georgia and Tennessee to New York, Ohio, and Pennsylvania. They are found in these areas mostly in the larger lakes and rivers, where they stay near weed beds, sunken logs, or near lily pads.

Muskies can be caught on a large variety of lures, such as big surface and underwater plugs, large spoons, and spinners. They also take natural baits such as minnows, suckers, and other small fish. These should be fished live, and the muskie should be given plenty of time to swallow the bait. Trolling is a good way to take muskies, and big plugs and spoons are the best lures to use for this type of fishing. Whichever method you use, make sure that your rod is fairly stiff and that the line is stronger than that used for ordinary freshwater fishing.

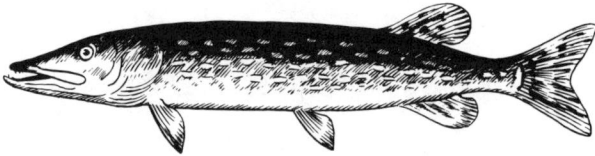

Pike

## PIKE

The pike is smaller than the muskellunge, usually running from 5 to 20 pounds in weight. The largest caught on rod and reel weighed 46 pounds, 2 ounces. However, pike are more plentiful than muskellunge, especially in Canada. In the United States, pike are found from New York through the Great Lakes to the upper Mississippi Valley. Although a pike looks something like a muskellunge in general body shape, it differs in coloring. A pike is usually a dark green or olive gray, with many light-yellow bean-shaped spots all over its body. The belly is yellow white.

## PICKEREL

The pickerel is the smallest member of the pike family. This fish looks like a small pike or muskellunge, but it never grows bigger than 9 or 10 pounds. Most pickerel caught are much smaller, usually running from 1 to 3 pounds.

The pickerel can be recognized by the "chain" markings found on its body. These are dark lines that look like links of a chain, overlaid on a background of greenish yellow.

Pickerel

Pickerel are usually found in the shallower parts of a lake and quieter parts of a river, where they like to lie among the weeds and lily pads.

You can catch pickerel on small plugs, spoons, spinners, and streamer flies. These can be cast or trolled behind a boat.

Another popular way to catch pickerel is with a long cane pole or fiberglass pole and a strip of pork rind on a hook. This is "skittered," or skipped, along the surface of the water among lily pads and other pickerel spots.

Pickerel are also caught with live minnows or frogs and a light float or bobber. When a pickerel grabs the bait, let him run with it until he stops and swallows it.

## Walleye

The walleye is sometimes called the walleyed pike, but it is actually a member of the perch family and is more closely related to the yellow perch than to the pike. The walleye has a large white eye that looks like glass. The body of this fish is dark olive green on the back and yellow on the sides. Most of the walleyes

Walleye

caught weigh from 2 to 5 pounds. However, they often reach more than 10 pounds and grow as big as 22 pounds.

The walleye is found in the eastern part of the United States and Canada, as far south as North Carolina, and also in the Great Lakes region and through the Mississippi Valley.

Walleyes prefer lakes and rivers with deep water and gravel, sand, or rock bottoms. In rivers, look for them in the deeper pools and eddies. In lakes they frequent rock and gravel bars that drop off to deeper water nearby. They also gather in areas where rivers or streams enter a lake.

Although you can catch walleyes all day long in deeper waters by trolling or still-fishing, best results are obtained by fishing early in the morning and toward evening. Walleyes are very active at night and come into shallow water after dark to feed. Fishing for walleyes is best early in the spring or late in the fall, when the water turns cold.

Walleyes can be caught on lures such as plugs, spoons, spinners, and jigs. They will also take natural baits such as minnows, lamprey eels, and big worms.

Slow trolling is one of the best ways to catch walleyes. A popular lure is a June Bug spinner, with a minnow or several worms on the hook. Walleyes will also strike plugs and spoons that are reeled deep and slow. In fact, most lures used for walleyes should be moved as deep and slowly as possible. You can also troll very slowly or drift with the wind using a big night crawler or leech on a sliding sinker rig along the bottom.

## Catfish

There are many kinds of catfish that can be caught in freshwater rivers and lakes. Some, like the bullheads or horned pouts, are small, rarely reaching more than a few pounds in weight. Others, like the blue catfish, have reached 150 pounds. Another large catfish is the flathead catfish, which may reach 100 pounds. One of the most popular catfish is the channel catfish, which grows to 58 pounds. The illustration below shows the bullhead, which is caught in many waters.

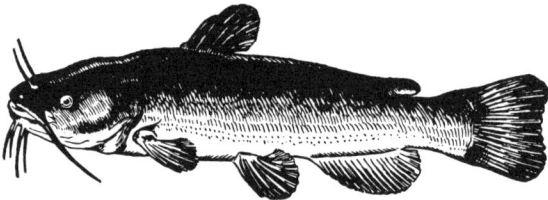

Bullhead

The larger catfish are found mostly in the Mississippi Valley region and other large reservoirs, lakes, and rivers. Bullheads are found mostly east of the Rockies and have also been introduced in the West, particularly in California.

Catfish are found in some lakes, but mostly frequent the larger, slow-moving rivers. They usually stay in the quiet, deep pools and eddies and below dams. Bullheads, like most catfish, bite best early in the morning, in the evening, and at night. The fishing is particularly good when the stream becomes muddy from recent rains.

Catfish are usually caught by still-fishing with hand lines or cane poles, or on rod and reel. They bite on many natural baits such as earthworms, minnows, pieces of fish, chunks of meat, and various "stink" baits made with combinations of cheese, ground meat, and flour. Even pieces of laundry soap on a hook have been used to catch catfish! For small catfish or bullheads use a No. 1/0 or 2/0 hook. For the larger catfish, sizes No. 5/0, 6/0, or 7/0 hooks are good. The Eagle Claw is a fine hook for catfish.

## Carp

At one time there were no carp in this country. Then they were sent from Europe and introduced into the eastern part of the United States in many rivers and lakes. Now carp have become so plentiful in the waters of many sections of the country that they are considered a pest.

The carp varies greatly in color, being yellowish, dark green, brown, or purplish black, depending on the water where it is found. In general shape, the carp looks like the common goldfish, which is actually a small carp. The carp has round lips like the sucker.

Most of the carp caught run from 2 to 8 pounds in weight. However, many carp weighing up to 15 or 20 pounds are caught, and they sometimes reach more than 50 pounds.

Carp can be found in many lakes, ponds, and rivers with mud bottoms and plenty of weeds or lily pads. In rivers they prefer the quieter pools and eddies. In lakes they often come close to shore to feed among the weeds. They can often be seen swimming near the surface or jumping out of the water with a loud splash.

Carp bite best during the late spring, summer, and early fall months. Fish for them early in the morning, in the evening, and at night.

Carp can be caught on almost any kind of fishing

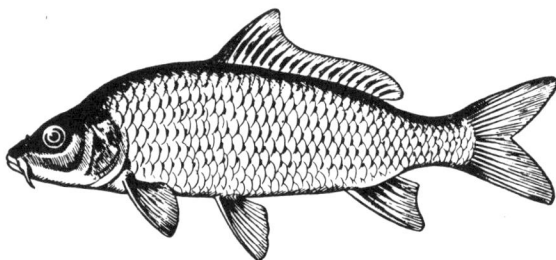

Carp

tackle: hand lines, bait-casting, spinning, spin-casting, and even light saltwater rods and reels. The best bait for carp is a doughball made from flour and cornmeal with a little bit of sugar or honey added. This is mixed with water and molded into a pear-shaped mass around a hook. The best hook to use is an Eagle Claw in sizes No. 1 or 1/0 for small carp and sizes No. 2/0 or 3/0 for big carp.

When fishing for carp make sure that the bait lies on the bottom. If you are fishing in a river with a strong current, you may have to use a sinker weighing 1 ounce or 2 to keep the bait on the bottom. For best results cast the bait out so that it is at least 30 or 40 feet from shore. Then sit down and wait for a bite. Do not walk around or make any disturbance. Carp are very sensitive and suspicious fish. If they see you they will not bite.

When a carp first picks up the bait you will notice the line moving slightly. Do not pick up the line or rod at this time. Wait until you see the line moving out at a fast speed before you try to set the hook. Carp fight hard and will often give you several runs before they are brought to shore.

# 9. Saltwater Bottom-Fishing Tackle

Saltwater bottom fishing is popular with millions of anglers. You will see these people fishing from boats, piers, docks, bridges, and shore. This is not surprising. Bottom fishing requires such simple fishing tackle and bait that it doesn't cost much compared to other types of saltwater fishing. Bottom fishing is also easy—almost anyone can catch a good mess of fish when they are running. And, finally, most fish caught by bottom fishing make good eating.

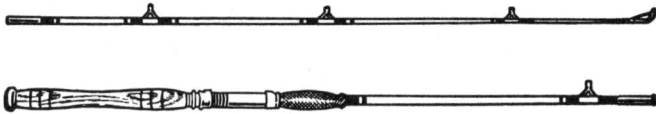

Two-piece boat rod

Saltwater bottom fishing is similar to freshwater still-fishing. In both types natural bait is used and is allowed to remain in the water at all times. The main difference is that in fresh water you often fish with a float to keep the bait off the bottom, whereas in saltwater bottom fishing, you keep the bait on or close to the bottom. You usually need heavy sinkers because of the deep water and strong tides.

## Rods

The best rod for bottom fishing is the saltwater boat rod, which comes in one or two sections and runs from 5 to 6 feet in overall length. Such a rod can be used from piers, bridges, boats, or shore. You can get either a solid fiberglass or hollow fiberglass boat rod for bottom fishing. These rods are ideal for boat fishing in deep water with heavy sinkers and for good-sized fish.

If you want to fish in shallow waters, such as saltwater bays, inlets, and rivers, you can get a lighter boat or bay rod, such as rods used for weakfish or flounders. These rods are thinner, more limber, and usually shorter.

Many anglers also use saltwater spinning rods and

surf rods for bottom fishing. These are fine if you are catching small fish in shallow water and using light sinkers, but when fishing in deep waters, where heavy sinkers are needed, a boat rod is more suitable. (See the drawing on page 113, which shows a saltwater boat rod.)

## Reels

Almost any of the smaller saltwater reels can be used for bottom fishing, but the saltwater bay or boat reels are best for this purpose. The smaller reels can be used for shallow water, while the larger reels are better for deeper waters and big fish. In very deep water, when going after big fish, anglers also use bigger ocean reels—Nos. 3/0 to 6/0—used for offshore trolling. The reel you use for bottom fishing should have a free-spool lever with which to disengage the spool, and a star drag to adjust the tension when fighting a big fish.

Bottom-fishing reel

## Lines

You can use braided nylon or Dacron lines, but more and more people are using monofilament nylon lines for bottom fishing. These lines are strong, waterproof, and almost invisible. Monofilament lines testing 20 or 25 pounds are used for shallow waters and small fish. For bigger fish in deeper waters and in rocky areas, monolines testing 30, 40, or 50 pounds are best.

## Sinkers

Sinkers are important in bottom fishing. They get the bait down to the bottom and hold it there despite the tide or current. Sinkers come in different sizes, shapes, and weights. Each is best suited for a particular kind of fishing and bottom.

The bank sinker, one of the most widely used, is good for bottom fishing over rocks or sandy bottoms. The diamond sinker, also popular, is widely used from boats in deep water. The square sinker also works well in deep water. The egg-shaped sinker, which has a hole

egg

bank          diamond          round

**Sinkers**

running through the middle, is used for wary fish that nibble at the bait. The line runs through this sinker, and the angler can feel the lightest bite, but the fish cannot feel the weight of the sinker. The round sinker is best when fishing over extremely rocky bottoms, where other types of sinkers get caught and are lost. Different weights of sinkers should be carried at all times. If the water is shallow and the tide is weak, sinkers in the lighter weights of 2, 3, or 4 ounces can be used. For deeper water and strong currents you may need sinkers weighing 6, 8, 10, or even 12 ounces.

# Hooks

Hooks are also important in bottom fishing. Many types of hooks are used, depending on the fish to be caught and the bait used. One of the most popular hooks for saltwater bottom fishing is the Eagle Claw pattern. The O'Shaughnessy hook is another popular pattern for medium-sized to large bottom fish. Other hooks often used are the Sproat, Carlisle, Pacific Bass, Virginia, and Chestertown. If you are not certain which hook to use for a certain fish, ask your local fishing-tackle dealer to recommend the best type and size.

# Rigs

The basic bottom-fishing rig consists of a sinker tied to the end of the line with hooks tied above the sinker. One or two hooks are usually used, but as many as four or five can be used.

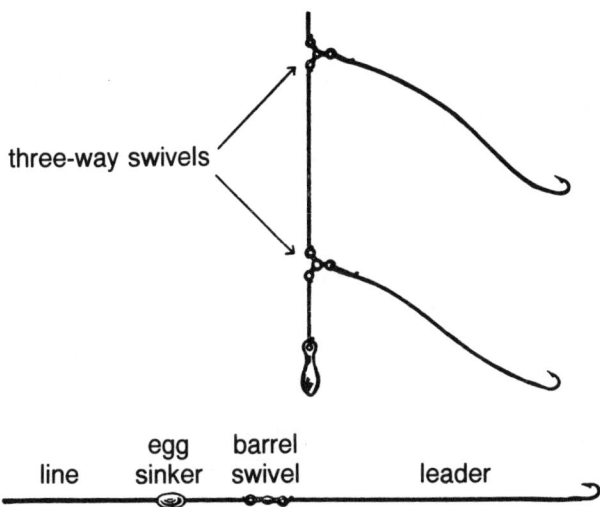

three-way swivels

line | egg sinker | barrel swivel | leader

Two bottom-fishing rigs

Another popular bottom-fishing rig makes use of an egg-shaped sinker. Here the hook is tied to one end of the nylon leader, while a barrel swivel is tied to the other end. Then the line is run through the hole in the egg-shaped sinker and is tied to the barrel swivel. The sinker slides up and down the fishing line. The drawing above shows these two bottom-fishing rigs.

You can make up such rigs by buying the eyed hooks, nylon leader material, swivels, and the sinkers separately.

## How to Bottom Fish

If you live near salt water you can find many spots where you can do bottom fishing. One of the best places is a pier or dock where you can go out and fish in deep water. Some of these piers are free to the public, while others are private and charge a small fee for fishing. Most of them are open all day and all night, have benches and shelters, and also sell or rent fishing tackle, bait, and soft drinks.

Most of the popular piers are crowded, and to get a good spot you have to come early in the morning. This is especially true when some kind of fish is running, and the news of good catches spreads. However, most fishing piers are fairly long and even the latecomers usually find a spot where they can squeeze in and fish.

Bridges are also good locations for bottom fishing, if fishing is allowed. If there is a sidewalk, fishing is usually safe; but on some bridges, where there is little room to stand, you have to watch out for moving autos and fishing can be dangerous. It doesn't pay to fish where there is danger of being hit by a car.

Bottom fishing is also done from the party or open boats or drift boats that leave from many cities and towns. Here you pay up to $12 to $15 a day for a day's fishing. The boat takes you out into deep water, where you anchor or drift with the tide and wind. These boats usually supply the bait at no extra charge. You can bring your own rod, reel, and line. But most of these boats also rent fishing rods and reels and sell hooks, sinkers, and rigs on board. Although some of these boats also sell food and drinks, it's a good idea to take your lunch with you.

You can also bottom fish from a rowboat or skiff in

many bays, sounds, and inlets. Such small boats can be rented in many places, with or without an outboard motor. In many places they will tow you out and bring you back from the fishing grounds if you rent a boat without a motor. Some anglers bring their own outboard motors because renting them can cost quite a bit. If the fishing spot is nearby, you can often row there, but if it is distant you need a motor to get there. You also have to buy your own bait, which is sold by most of the fishing stations that rent boats and motors.

You can also do some bottom fishing from shore, jetties, or beaches. This is similar to surf-fishing and will be covered in the chapter on surf-fishing tackle.

Bottom fishing is a more sociable type of fishing than other kinds of saltwater angling. Bottom anglers often gather in groups or fleets of boats at certain spots and fish near each other. That is one of the best ways to locate a good bottom-fishing spot. If you see many anglers or boats in one spot, it's a good idea to try fishing there too. In most cases they are catching fish, and you can join in the fun. Of course, you won't get so close that you interfere with the other anglers' fishing.

If you go out on a party boat or drift boat, the captain will take you to the best fishing grounds. If you rent a small boat the owner or manager of the place will direct you to the most productive fishing spots.

Bottom fish usually gather where there is plenty of food for them. They eat worms, crabs, clams, mussels, oysters, and small fish. These are found around sunken wrecks, coral reefs, mussel and oyster beds, rocks, and seaweed.

If you are fishing from an anchored boat or from shore, cast or let the baited hook and sinker sink down to the bottom. The sinker should be heavy enough to stay on the bottom in the tide or current. When you get a bite, let the fish nibble a while until you feel a strong pull, then jerk hard with the rod tip to set the hook. Sometimes the fish bite better if you move the bait. To do this, lift the sinker from the bottom and then let it drop back again. Let the sinker lie on the bottom a few seconds, and then lift it once again. Keep doing this regularly. If the tide is very strong you may have to let out a few feet of line each time you let the sinker drop back. If you don't feel the bottom you may have to change to a heavier sinker.

You can also bottom fish by drifting in a boat, letting it move with the tide and wind. The sinker bounces along the bottom, and you cover a lot of territory, at the same time moving the bait along the bottom to attract fish.

# 10. Saltwater Spinning Tackle

Saltwater spinning tackle has become very popular with people who fish from boats, piers, bridges, jetties, shore, and surf. Saltwater spinning tackle offers many advantages. The rods and reels are simple to operate, casting is easy, there are no backlashes and no spooling of the line by hand. Spinning outfits are usually light and provide a lot of sport with even the smallest fish.

There are many saltwater spinning rods and reels to

choose from. Because spinning tackle is expensive to buy, it is important to find out what kind of fishing you plan to do before choosing a saltwater spinning outfit.

# Rods

Saltwater spinning rods come in three weights— light, medium, and heavy. The light rod can be a heavy type freshwater spinning rod, but for best results get one built for saltwater fishing. Such a rod can be cast with one hand and should be from 6 to 7 feet long. It should handle fishing lures of weights up to 1½ ounces. You can use such a rod from a boat or shore for casting light lures and for catching smaller fish up to 20 pounds in weight.

The medium-weight saltwater spinning rod runs from 7½ to 9 feet in overall length. It has a fairly long butt section so that it can be cast with two hands. It should be able to handle lures weighing up to 2 ounces and sinkers up to 3 or 4 ounces. You can use such a rod from boats, piers, bridges, shore, jetties, or surf for fish of varying weights up to 40 or 50 pounds.

The heavy spinning rod is used mostly for fishing from piers, shore, or the surf where long casts are needed and big fish such as striped bass and channel bass up to 50 or 60 pounds may be caught.

# Reels

Saltwater spinning reels are very similar to freshwater spinning reels, except that they are usually larger and stronger, in order to stand up in saltwater fishing; they hold more line, and they fight the bigger fish. The metal parts of a saltwater spinning reel shouldn't rust or corrode. The bail and roller of such a reel should be made of a hard material and should operate efficiently. The reel should also have a smooth, dependable drag.

A good way to buy a saltwater spinning reel is to get an experienced fishing friend to advise you which reel to get. If this angler has used a certain spinning reel for several seasons, you can be pretty sure that the reel is sturdy and dependable.

Saltwater spinning reels come in two or three sizes, from a small size, which is suitable for use with a light spinning rod, up to the largest sizes, which are best with heavy spinning rods and heavy lines usually used for big fish.

Saltwater spinning reel

# Lines

Saltwater spinning lines are usually made from synthetics such as nylon and are called monofilament or monolines. For the light saltwater spinning outfit, lines testing from 6 to 10 pounds are best. For the medium-weight spinning outfit, lines testing from 10 to 15 pounds can be used, while the heavier spinning outfits call for lines testing from 15 to 25 pounds.

To take the shock of casting and wear and tear around rocks and sand, most saltwater anglers tie a heavier monoleader to the end of their line. This should be at least 10 or 12 feet long so that a few turns of the leader go on the reel when you are ready to cast. It should also be a few pounds stronger than the main fishing line on the reel.

You should also carry at least one or two extra spools filled with the same line you already have on the reel. Or you can carry lighter or heavier line if you feel you may need it.

# Accessories

When fishing with spinning tackle in salt water, you need a tackle box to keep your lures; sinkers; hooks; extra reel, spool, or line; and other equipment. For boat fishing a big tackle box with compartments for fishing lures and other items is best. But make sure that it is made for saltwater fishing, since the small boxes made for freshwater fishing aren't large enough and they usually rust or corrode when they are wet or dampened with salt water.

If you are fishing from the surf a shoulder bag or small pouches carried on a belt are better than a tackle box, since they leave your hands free for carrying other gear. You also need boots or waders. These are discussed in more detail in the following chapter.

The artificial lures and natural baits used in saltwater spin fishing are also covered in chapters 15 and 16.

## How to Spin Cast

Casting with a light one-handed saltwater spinning rod is similar to casting with a freshwater spinning rod. When you use the longer, heavier spinning rods, however, two hands are necessary in casting. You go through the same motions as with a one-handed rod, but you use two hands on the handle or butt for more power and speed. The right hand grips the butt or reel seat above the reel, while the left hand holds the end of the butt. Then you bring the rod back over your head and stop it when it reaches a point directly over your head or slightly behind it. Immediately you start the forward cast, snapping the rod sharply in front of you toward the target. To complete the cast you follow through and release the line from your forefinger, letting the lure shoot toward the spot you want to hit. To stop the cast you place your forefinger on the reel spool.

# 11. Surf-fishing Tackle

Surf-fishing offers some of the most exciting and satisfying fishing that can be done in salt water. There is something fascinating about casting into the breaking waves from the beach. Many people who have never caught fish from the surf find it hard to believe that big fish will come so close to shore. But every year quite a few striped bass and channel bass weighing 40, 50 pounds, or more are caught near the beach. Not to mention sharks weighing 100 to 500 pounds!

Of course, surf-fishing isn't easy, and you don't catch as many fish as in other forms of saltwater fishing. But most surf anglers would rather catch one fish from the surf than ten from a boat. When you cast into the ocean with a lure or bait, you never know for sure what you will hook. It may be a small 1-pound whiting or a monster shark. But no matter what you hook, you will get a good fight on the end of your line. Most fish found and caught in the surf are powerful and put up a satisfying fight.

Surf-fishing is also one of the least expensive forms of saltwater fishing, once you buy the tackle. You do not have to rent or charter a boat. You do not have to fish from a special location such as a pier or bridge. Instead, you have miles of beach or shoreline where you can practice surf-fishing, coming and going as you please. Such freedom of choice and convenience appeal to many men, women, and young people.

But to catch fish in the surf you must start off with the proper tackle. If you have a friend who does surf-fishing, ask this person to help you select the best outfit for the area you plan to fish. However, if you have no such friend, the following information will help you select the proper outfit.

## Rods

Two types of outfits are used for surf-fishing: saltwater spinning tackle and conventional surf tackle. Casting with a spinning reel is easier than with a conventional reel, so most surf anglers prefer a spinning rod and reel for their fishing. The spinning rod you need for surf-fishing is the medium or heavy saltwater rod described in the previous chapter. It will range from 9 to 12 feet in overall length and should have a fairly long handle, or butt.

The conventional surf rod has smaller guides or rings and is usually stiffer than a spinning rod. The best rod of this type to get is the medium-weight surf rod, which has a tip section from 6½ to 7½ feet in length. The butt, or handle, can be anywhere from 22 to 28 inches long. Such a rod should be able to cast lures up to 3 ounces and sinkers up to 5 ounces.

# Reels

If you have a surf spinning rod you will get a large, saltwater spinning reel to go with it. If you buy a conventional surf rod you will need a conventional revolving-spool reel. These reels have light plastic or metal spools, a star drag, free spool, and a fast gear ratio of at least 3 to 1. They come in two or three different sizes, holding anywhere from 150 to 250 yards of 25- to 36-pound-test line. The 200-yard surf reel is best for the medium-weight surf rod.

# Lines

If you are using spinning tackle in the surf, you will need monofilament line testing anywhere from 15 to 25 pounds. The lighter lines are used with light lures and

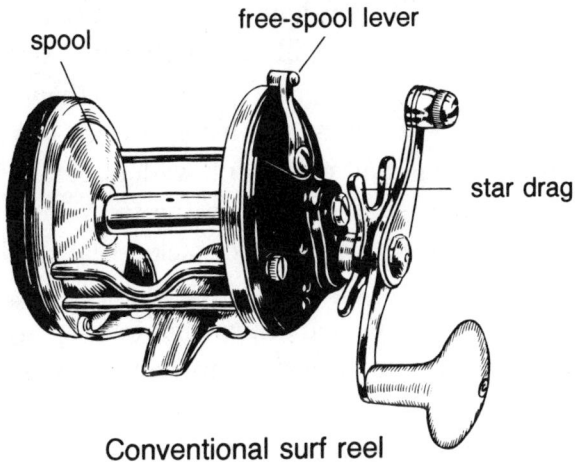

Conventional surf reel

light spinning rods. The stronger lines are used with medium or heavy spin rods and heavy lures or sinkers.

For conventional surf reels you need either nylon or Dacron braided surf-fishing line. Dacron lines are slightly thinner than nylon lines, which means that you can get a bit more line on your reel. Most surf anglers use lines testing 30 or 36 pounds with their conventional rods and reels. Some anglers also use monofilament line testing 30 pounds on their conventional surf reels, but these can give you some trouble when casting.

## Accessories

The surf angler finds that he also needs a pair of boots or waders, especially when fishing in cold northern waters early in the spring, late in the fall, or at night. If you will be fishing mostly from sandy beaches or jetties, hip boats will be satisfactory especially if you also wear waterproof pants over them. But for fishing in spots where you have to wade out into the water, you will find waist-high waders better. Waders are also warmer if you fish in the fall.

You also need a waterproof jacket that can be worn over the waders. Such a jacket or parka has a hood, waterproof seams, and drawstring or snap around the neck and waist to keep the water out when waves rise or break.

You will also want a canvas shoulder bag to carry lures, sinkers, hooks, extra line or reel, and other equipment if you plan to fish mostly in one spot all day. If, however, you plan to fish many spots or walk long distances along a beach, you will find a belt with small pouches or bags for holding lures much better. The best type of belt for this is the pistol belt, which is sold in many Army-Navy surplus stores. This belt has many holes to which you can attach small bags or pouches.

Surf anglers also use a gaff, a big hook attached to a handle, for landing a fish when it is close to shore. For fishing from rock jetties you need a gaff with a handle at least 6 to 8 feet long. If you are fishing from a beach, you can use a gaff that has a shorter handle. The illustration shows these two types of gaffs.

For night fishing, surf anglers also need a flashlight or headlight of some sort. A headlight that can be worn around the neck or head is most convenient, since it

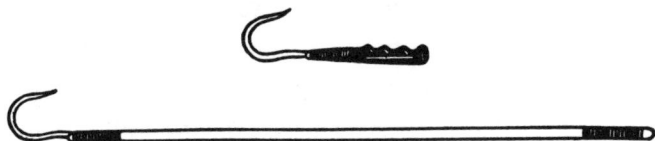

**Gaffs**

leaves your hands free for casting or putting bait on the hook.

For fishing from sandy beaches with bait, a sand spike is needed. This is nothing more than a big hollow metal or plastic tube with a pointed prong or end that is stuck into the sand. The rod butt is pushed into the hole of this tube to hold the rod up and keep the reel away from the sand.

Other items often needed in surf-fishing are a knife, sunglasses, a can of oil for the reel, and, of course, extra sinkers, swivels, hooks, and rigs. A folding chair is also handy to have if you are fishing with bait and have long waits for a bite.

## How to Surf Cast

If you have a spinning outfit you can follow the instructions in chapter 10.

When casting with a conventional surf rod and reel, stand with your feet well apart and face down the beach, with the water on your left. Your left foot is forward, pointing toward the ocean. Your right foot points down the beach. Now set the reel at free spool.

Place your right thumb on the reel spool and grip the butt of the rod with your left hand. Start with the rod extending back over your right shoulder. Then, with a quick snap, bring the rod tip over your head. Pull down with your left hand and thrust the butt forward with your right hand. Twist your body to face the target. When the rod tip passes a point directly over your head, remove your thumb from the reel spool for a second. As the line starts to run off, put your thumb back on the spool. Keep it there lightly at all times now. If the line runs off too fast apply a bit more pressure with your thumb. As the lure reaches the target and begins dropping, you stop the cast by pressing hard on the spool with your thumb.

To become a good surf caster with conventional tackle requires practice until you can feel the line moving out at the proper speed. Your thumb must act like a brake—applying pressure on the spool if it's going too fast and easing up if the spool slows down. After a while your timing and thumb pressure will become automatic, and casting will be easier. But in the beginning do not try to cast too far. It is important to cast smoothly and accurately.

# 12. Offshore Fishing Tackle

This chapter covers offshore fishing, which is also called big-game and deep-sea fishing. In this fishing you go out in boats anywhere from 18 to 50 feet long. These boats go offshore or out into the open ocean where they troll or drift for big-game fish. They often fish for such monsters of the deep as swordfish, marlin, tuna, and sharks, some of which may weigh several hundred pounds. However, offshore boats also catch smaller fish such as dolphin, wahoo, bonito, and small tuna.

Of course, to do offshore fishing you need a boat. If you have a friend or relative who owns such a boat, you may be invited to go out fishing in it. If you have to rent a boat it costs less if three or four people get together and share the cost of a boat. In some places boats can be rented for half a day, but usually the distant fishing grounds call for a full-day rental.

If you charter a boat, the captain usually supplies the fishing tackle and lures or baits, so you don't have to buy a rod, reel, line, or lures or baits. This is a good thing, because not many young people can afford to buy an offshore rod, reel, and line. Such tackle is expensive, and it is foolish to invest up to $200 or $300 for an offshore outfit that you may use only once or twice a year.

Offshore rods are made of solid fiberglass or hollow

Offshore-fishing reel

fiberglass and have strong guides, usually of the roller type. They also have strong reel seats and thick butts, or handles. The reels are large, with powerful drags and big spools that hold plenty of line. Lines used on offshore fish are made either of monofilament or braided Dacron and test anywhere from 20 to 130 pounds, depending on the size of the rod and reel you are using and the size of the fish you expect to catch.

Long cable or single-strand wire leaders up to 15 feet long are used in offshore fishing. They come in various thicknesses and strengths from 27 to 480 pounds. In recent years more and more anglers have been using strong monofilament leaders in these strengths.

The boats equipped for offshore fishing have outriggers, which are two very long poles on both sides of the boat. These can be spread out on both sides, and the fishing line can be attached to each outrigger by means of a clothespinlike device. When a fish hits the bait or lure, the line jumps out of the clothespin and drops into the water with plenty of slack or loose line allowing the fish time to swallow the bait. Outriggers also keep the lines apart when they are trolled. So you can troll more fishing lines at the same time, they don't tangle with each other, and they stay away from the white water, or wake, of the boat.

Most offshore fishing boats or sportfishing cruisers have a fishing chair or fighting chair, in which you can sit when you fight a fish. These chairs have a footrest and turn around so that you always face the fish during the fight. The chairs also have rod holders, metal tubes into which the rod is placed when you are not holding it.

For most offshore fishing you use whole fish, strips of fish, or other rigged baits. They are rigged with one or two large hooks. These combinations are prepared in advance and kept frozen until used.

You can also use artificial lures such as feather or nylon jigs, spoons, wooden plugs, or various plastic lures when trolling offshore. In recent years more and more big marlin, tuna, and sailfish have been caught on plastic squid, fish, or skirted lures rather than on natural baits.

When you go offshore fishing with a friend, relative, or charter boat captain, follow this person's advice. You may troll the bait or lure all day and get only one or two strikes from big fish. You must know what to do at this time or you will fail to hook the fish. If you follow instructions carefully, in most cases you will succeed.

The same thing holds true when you are fighting a big fish on the end of the line. Listen to what the captain, mate, or fishing friend or relative says and follow whatever advice is offered. In fighting a big fish, the secret is not to let the fish rest, but to keep him on the move as much as possible. When a fish is first hooked it should be allowed to run or jump freely. If the fish stops, you can start bringing him toward the boat. This is done by lowering the rod and reeling in line. Then lean back and raise the rod and try to move the fish toward you. Then lower the rod again, reel in line, and then lean back and pull again. Keep repeating this as long as the fish is coming slightly your way. When the fish starts running again, let him go and stop pumping or trying to regain line. When he stops, you begin pumping once more. Do not touch the drag or brake on the reel, unless you are told to do so. Usually when you get the fish near the boat, you may have to tighten the drag a bit, but not too much, because if the fish starts running suddenly, he may break the line or pull out the hook.

Offshore fishing can be uncomfortable if the water is rough. If you are bothered by seasickness, get some antinausea pills from your doctor or druggist. There are several kinds available.

It may take many trips before you are lucky enough to hook and land a big-game fish. However, once you do you will feel it was all worthwhile, and you will start fishing all over again for a still bigger fish or a different kind. There are always bigger fish offshore than have been caught so far.

# 13. Saltwater Baits

In saltwater fishing most anglers use natural baits to catch fish. From giant tuna to tiny porgies, most saltwater fish will take a properly presented natural bait. This means that the angler who knows most about natural saltwater baits—how they are caught, how they are hooked and rigged, and how they are presented—will catch the most and biggest fish.

Some of these natural baits you can obtain yourself

if you spend some time and energy. Other saltwater baits can be bought from coastal fishing tackle stores or bait dealers. The kind of bait you use will depend mostly on the fish you seek and the bait that is producing best at the time. It is always a good idea to find out which bait has been catching the most fish recently. It is also a good idea to take two or three different kinds of bait on a fishing trip. The following natural baits are the most popular.

## Sea Worms

Sea worms are effective bait for many saltwater fish. Two kinds of worms are generally used along the Atlantic coast. One is the clam worm, often called the sandworm. It has a blue or green back and pink or red undersides and "legs."

The other worm is the bloodworm, which is pink or flesh colored and has a smooth body tapering to a point on both ends. When touched or disturbed it shoots out a long head with four tiny, black jaws.

Clam worms and bloodworms can be dug at low tide in many bays with mud flats. You can use a clam hoe or a garden fork to dig the worms from the mud. But it is hard work, so most anglers would rather buy the worms by the dozen from a fishing tackle store.

When using worms for bait for big fish such as striped bass, place a whole worm or even two or three worms on a hook. For smaller fish such as flounders, porgies, and croakers, cut the worm into three or four

bloodworm

clam worm

Sea worms and methods of hooking

pieces and use a small piece on the hook. The drawing shown here illustrates the way to put worms on a hook.

## Clams

There are many kinds of clams that can be used for bait. Some are big, like the surf or sea clam, often called the "skimmer" clam. This clam lives in the sand along the beaches of the Atlantic coast near shore and in deeper water. After a storm or heavy sea these clams are often washed up on the beach and can be picked up at low tide. You can also buy these clams from fishing tackle stores and bait dealers located near the ocean.

Another clam that can be used for bait is the hard

Clam and method of hooking

clam, which is found in most bays. These clams are smaller and are usually sold in restaurants and fish markets. You can also obtain them by feeling for them in shallow water with your bare feet when the tide is low. Or you can rake them out of the sand with a clam hoe, either wading in shallow water or leaning from the sides of a boat in deeper water.

The soft meaty part of the clam is used for bait. You can open clams by inserting a knife between the shells or by cracking them against a rock or other hard surface. The meat inside can be cut up into small sections for small fish, or you can use the entire insides of a clam for big fish. Run the hook through the clam meat two or three times if you are using the whole clam. Run it once if you are using a small piece. See the illustration here.

## Squid

The squid is a relative of the octopus, which is widely used for fish bait. Squid bait is tough, white, and stays on a hook for a long time. Most of all, saltwater fish like

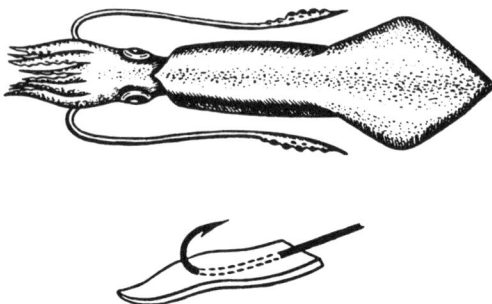

Squid and method of hooking

it. Sometimes squid are washed ashore and can be picked up at low tide, but usually they are bought from tackle stores, bait dealers, or fish markets. Nowadays they are frozen in 1-pound packages and sold for bait. If you buy the squid fresh they should be kept on ice until used.

Squid are cleaned by removing the insides and the thin skin around the body. Then they are cut into strips or small pieces for most of the smaller fish. For big fish such as striped bass, a whole squid or the head is often used for bait.

## Menhaden

The menhaden, or mossbunker, is a fish which is often used for bait and chum, which are bits of bait spread on the water to attract fish. Called bunker for short, this fish is very oily and is ground up and thrown into the water to attract larger fish. The oil and pieces of menhaden spread out and create a "slick," which

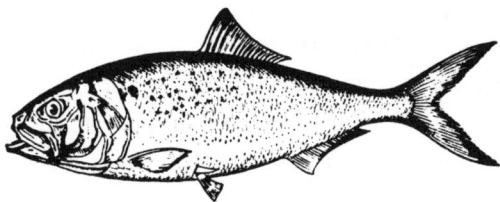

**Menhaden**

draws fish near the boat. This is done when fishing for bluefish, tuna, bonito, albacore, and sharks.

The menhaden also makes good bait if it is cut into chunks and placed on a hook. It can be used for striped bass, bluefish, weakfish, channel bass, and other fish. Menhaden have also been used alive to catch big striped bass, bluefish, tuna, and sharks.

## Silversides

The silversides, also called a spearing, is another small baitfish used in saltwater fishing. It is found close to shore in the surf, in bays, inlets, and saltwater creeks and rivers. You can catch silversides with a seine or other net, but most fishermen buy them in a fishing tackle store, or from a bait dealer. They are used on a hook to catch silver hake or whiting, bluefish, weakfish, mackerel, fluke, and other fish.

## Sand Eel

The sand eel, or sand launce, is another generally small, useful baitfish. It is a long, slim fish that looks like a tiny eel. Sand eels are sometimes caught in the wet sand along beaches. But most of them are bought from fishing tackle stores or bait dealers. They make good bait for silver hake or whiting, bluefish, striped bass, fluke, and other fish. Hook a sand eel through the eye and then in the middle of the body.

## Killifish

The killifish, or mummichog, often called killie for short, is a popular bait for fluke or summer flounders. It is sold alive at fishing tackle stores and bait dealers. You can catch your own killies in a minnow trap baited with crushed crabs, clams, or mussels. Killies live a long time if they are hooked through the lips as shown in the illustration. Killies are kept alive in small boxes or cages submerged in the water. Besides fluke you can catch small bluefish, sea bass, and weakfish with killies.

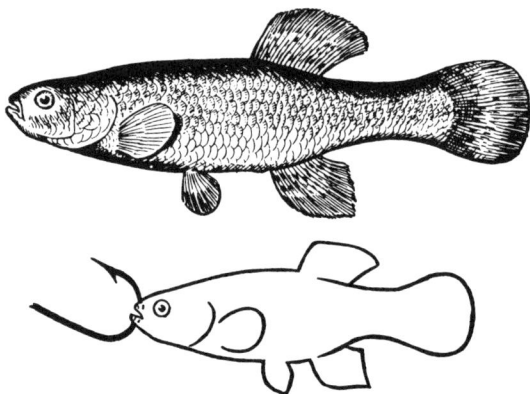

Killifish and method of hooking

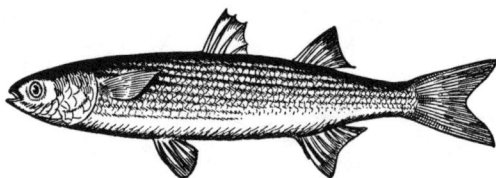

**Mullet**

## Mullet

The mullet is another widely used baitfish especially in Florida and other southern waters. Mullet are found swimming close to shore in large schools. Here they are caught in long seines or with cast nets. Mullet are also sold by bait dealers, fishing tackle stores, and in fish markets. The large mullet are cut up into chunks or strips before being placed on a hook, while the smaller mullet can be used whole. Mullet will catch striped bass, bluefish, channel bass, weakfish, tarpon, snappers, and many other saltwater fish.

## Crabs

There are many kinds of crabs that can be used for bait. Three of the most commonly used are the blue crab, the green crab, and the fiddler crab. The blue crab is the big crab often sold in restaurants and fish markets. For bait the best blue crabs are not the hard ones. You should try to get the shedder, or soft-shell, crabs. A shedder, or "peeler," crab has a hard shell, but if you break it the newly formed soft shell is underneath. A soft-shell crab already has thrown off its hard shell and

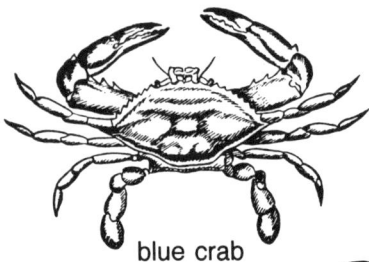

green crab

blue crab

fiddler crab

Crabs

is waiting for the new one to get hard. Both of these stages of the blue crab make good bait. You can sometimes catch the blue crabs with a long-handled crab net in shallow water in bays. You can use a whole crab for big fish such as striped bass or channel bass. Smaller pieces are used for weakfish, bluefish, whiting, and other fish. You may have to tie the crab around the hook with fine sewing thread to keep it from falling off the hook.

The green crab, found around rocks and jetties, is used for blackfish, or tautog. You can find this crab by turning over the smaller rocks at low tide. The larger green crabs are cut in half or quartered, while the smaller ones are used whole.

Fiddler crabs are found in holes in bay marshes that have mud and sandy bottoms. Two kinds are commonly used for bait: the dark-green "mud fiddler" and the tan-colored or lighter "china-back" fiddler. You can catch fiddlers at low tide by scooping them up with a net or hand before they hide in their holes. They are also sold in many fishing tackle stores.

## Shrimp

In Florida and other southern waters, live shrimp are used for bait to catch many kinds of fish. These shrimp are sold by fishing tackle stores and bait dealers and are kept in a container filled with salt water until used. They are hooked through the tail or back for best results. You can also use dead shrimp that have

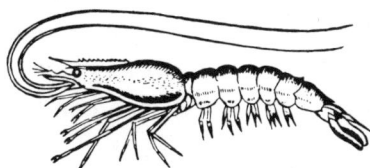

common shrimp

grass shrimp

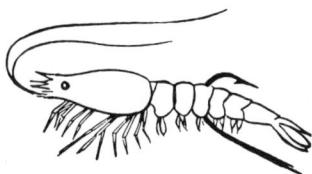

two grass shrimp
on a hook

Shrimp and methods of hooking

been frozen or kept on ice. Shrimp will catch sea trout; channel bass, or redfish; snappers; snook; and many other fish in southern waters.

In northern waters a smaller variety of shrimp known as the grass shrimp or common prawn is used for chum and bait. These small shrimp are used mainly for striped bass and weakfish, which are attracted to the boat by chumming. Here you throw three or four of the shrimp into the water at regular intervals. Then you can bait a hook with the same shrimp by placing two, three, or four of them on one hook. Other fish caught on these tiny shrimp include flounders, porgies, blackfish, and sea bass. The illustration (page 147) shows the two kinds of shrimp and how they are hooked.

This covers most of the important baits used in salt-water fishing. There are many others that can be found or bought and used at times. In fact, almost any small fish, shellfish or baitfish or a piece of big fish can be tried as bait.

# 14. Saltwater Lures

Many of the lures that are used in freshwater fishing can also be used for saltwater fishing. However, as a general rule, saltwater lures are heavier, stronger, and larger than freshwater types. The following lures are used in saltwater fishing.

## Spoons

There are many sizes, shapes, and weights of spoons used for saltwater fishing. They come in brass, copper, nickel, chrome, and painted finishes. The most popular

Saltwater spinner

finish for saltwater fishing is a nickel- or chrome-plated spoon. Some spoons are also made from stainless steel. Saltwater spoons run from the small 2-inch size up to large 12-inch spoons. These big spoons, often called bunker spoons, are used when trolling for big striped bass, bluefish, and other large saltwater fish. Although some of the smaller spoons may be equipped with treble hooks, most saltwater spoons have a strong single hook attached.

Spinners aren't used as often in saltwater fishing as in freshwater, and when they are used there is usually some kind of bait on the hook. One of the most popular types of saltwater spinner is the Cape Cod spinner, which has blades shaped like a willow leaf. This spinner is trolled slowly for striped bass or weakfish in bays and inlets. Two or more bloodworms or sandworms are usually placed on the hook behind the spinner. Other spinners used in saltwater fishing are the fluke and snapper spinners, which have two blades and a single hook. A small baitfish is usually put on the hook.

## Plugs

Wooden and plastic plugs are popular in saltwater fishing. There are many types of plugs in different sizes, shapes, weights, and actions. The plugs can be divided into two groups: surface and underwater types. The surface plugs include poppers, swimmers, and darters. These are reeled in on top of the water and create a disturbance or splash that makes them look like crippled baitfish. They imitate such small fish as menhaden, mullet, herring, and silversides.

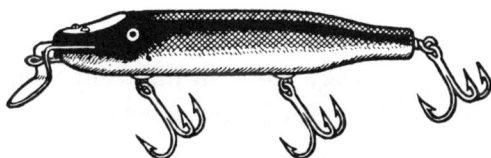

Underwater plugs used in salt water have metal lips or shapes that cause them to dive and dart or wriggle under the water. The color of the plug used is not too important in surface types, but should be considered in underwater models. The underwater plugs having a blue-mullet or a silver-mullet finish are good for most saltwater fish.

Both surface and underwater plugs for saltwater

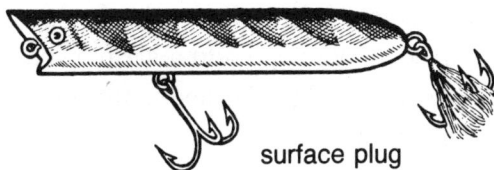

surface plug

underwater plug

Saltwater plugs

fishing come in various sizes, from small 3-inch lengths up to 12 inches. The small plugs are good for small fish and light tackle, while the heavier models are used for large fish and heavy tackle.

## Metal Squids

Metal squids have been used to catch fish in the surf for many years. They can also be used for casting or trolling from a boat. Metal squids come in different shapes, sizes, and weights; some are short and broad, others are long and slim. They all imitate some small fish found in salt water. The best metal squids were formerly made from block tin, but nowadays they are made from other metals. Some metal squids have bucktail hair or feathers wound around the hook. Some squids have a hook molded right into the body of the lure. Others have a free-swinging hook. Squids can be used plain also, or you can add a strip of pork rind or a plastic worm or tail to the hook. Most metal squids weigh from 1 to 3 ounces.

## Jigs

Jigs are also called bucktails, bugeyes, bullheads, and barracudas. They come in different weights, colors, and sizes. Jigs have heavy heads made from lead or other metal, and skirts of feathers, hair, nylon, or plastic wrapped around the hook. Some jigs also have plastic worms or tails or grubs on the hook. The metal head can be chrome-plated or painted in any color. Most jigs used in saltwater fishing have silver, white,

Saltwater jigs

or yellow heads and white or yellow skirts of bucktail or feathers. Some jigs also have plastic tails that look like shrimp.

The smaller, lighter jigs with small hooks are used with light fishing tackle. The larger, heavier jigs with big hooks are used with heavy fishing tackle and for trolling. Jigs can be cast or trolled behind a boat to catch many saltwater fish. They can also be bounced up and down on the bottom to catch many fish that are usually caught on natural baits.

Formerly small, natural eels were rigged with two hooks and used to catch striped bass. Nowadays plastic eels are used more often than the natural eels. Lures made from the skin from an eel are still used to a certain extent to catch striped bass and bluefish.

# 15. Making Saltwater Lures

As is the case with freshwater lures, many of the salt-water lures described in the previous chapter can be made at home. You not only save money, but also have a delightful hobby during the winter when fishing is slow. The fishing lures you make in advance will re-place those you lose during the coming fishing season.

When making spinners and spoons for saltwater fishing, you can follow most of the instructions in chap-ter 7 for making freshwater lures. The only difference is that in making saltwater spinners and spoons you usually use larger and stronger hooks, heavier wire, and larger spinner blades and spoons.

## Making Saltwater Plugs

You can also follow the instructions for making freshwater plugs in chapter 7 when making saltwater types. While plugs used in saltwater require stronger hooks and longer, heavier screw eyes, freshwater plugs in the bait-casting class are just right in size for casting with a light saltwater spinning outfit.

If, however, you plan to use the plugs for surf-fishing with heavy tackle for big fish, you will have to make them larger and heavier. These can be twice as long and thicker than those used for freshwater fishing.

One plug that can be made for saltwater fishing is the surface popper shown in the illustration. This plug should be about 6½ inches long and about 1⅛ inches thick. The head is cut at a 45-degree angle as shown.

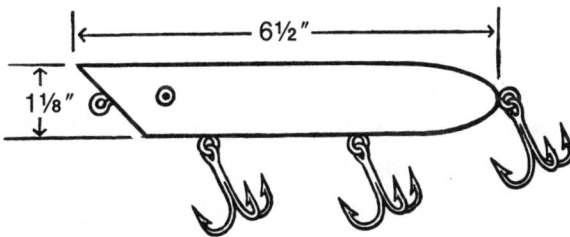

Surface popper

It should have three No. 5/0 treble hooks attached. Try to get extra-strong treble hooks when you make this plug. Many saltwater fish are big and powerful, and will straighten out ordinary thin-wire treble hooks. The same is true of the screw eyes you use on saltwater plugs. Try to get large, heavy-wire screw eyes made from brass or galvanized iron. You can use ordinary iron screw eyes, but these eventually rust away.

Cedar wood can be used to make saltwater plugs although it is light in weight. To make heavier plugs, which are easier to cast, you can use birch, fir, maple, or walnut.

To form a wood plug use a saw, rasp, and coarse file to shape the body. Then take a smooth file and sandpaper to finish it. Of course, if you are lucky enough to have a small wood lathe and other power tools at home, you can shape the plugs much faster. However, it is surprising how quickly you can turn out the plugs with ordinary hand tools after you make a few of them. You can also order ready-made wood and plastic plug bodies from some of the mail-order houses listed at the end of chapter 7.

## Making Jigs

Jigs are effective in both fresh and saltwater fishing. They are usually fished deep, near the bottom where they often get hung up and lost. By making your own jigs you can always have plenty on hand.

You can easily make a plaster mold to pour these

lures in large numbers. The first step in making one is to get a pattern or model to copy. You can buy a jig in a fishing tackle store for this, or you can carve out a pattern from soft wood.

The next step is to get a small cardboard box and pour in enough plaster of paris to fill it halfway. Then you smear the jig pattern to be copied with Vaseline, and press it halfway into the wet plaster. Then take two nails and sink them into the wet plaster, as shown in *A* on the following page. These nails will act as locating pins when you pour the jigs.

After the first half of the plaster mold hardens, brush the entire surface with heavy oil. Then mix more plaster of paris and pour it into the box to the top. When this plaster hardens, break up the cardboard box with a knife blade and separate the two plaster halves, removing the jig pattern. Then set the two plaster halves (casts) aside to dry for a week or even two weeks. After they are dry you carve out pouring holes and a slot to take the hook as shown in *B*. You can also cut a groove to take a wire eyelet. You can form such a wire eye from brass or copper wire.

Next, place a hook in the slot and the wire eyelet in its groove *(C)*. Then get some lead and melt it in a ladle over a gas or electric stove. Now you are ready to put the two plaster casts together and pour your jigs *(D)*. When you do this be very careful not to spill any hot lead on yourself, and make sure that the plaster cast is thoroughly dry, or else the hot lead will shoot out

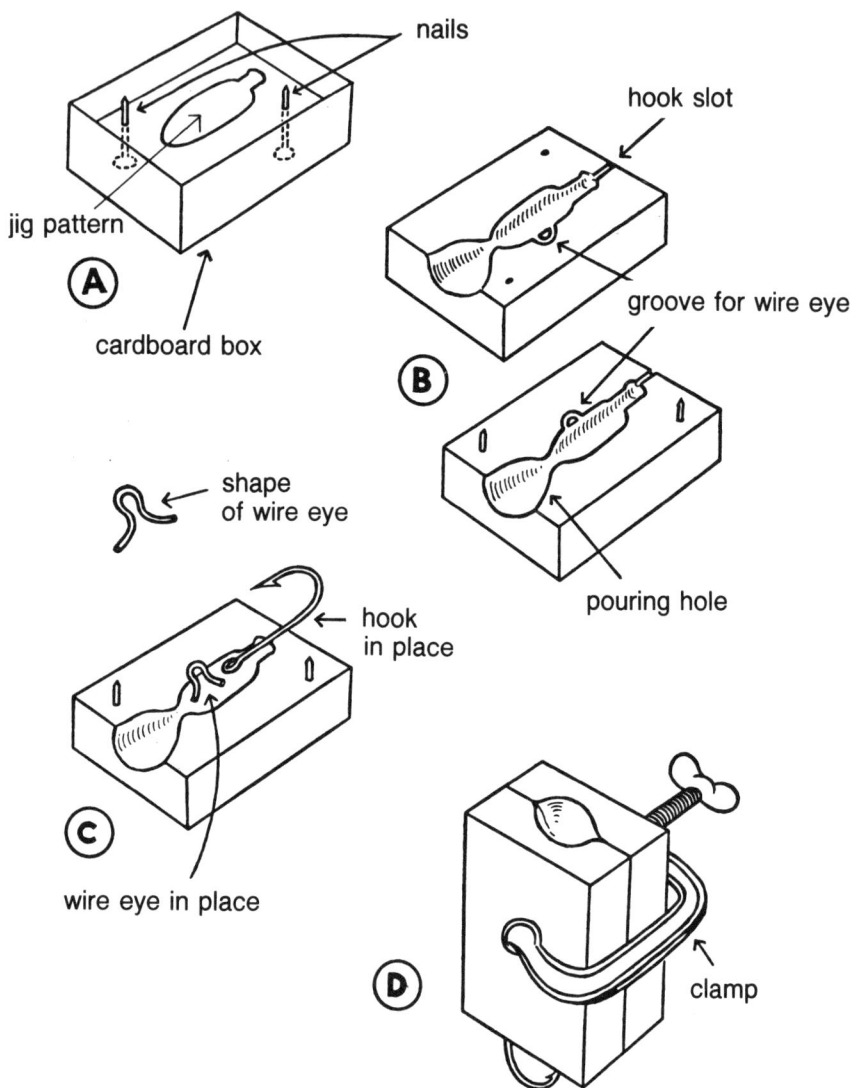

nails

jig pattern

hook slot

(A)

cardboard box

groove for wire eye

(B)

shape
of wire eye

pouring hole

hook
in place

(C)

wire eye in place

(D)

clamp

Making plaster mold for jigs

and spatter all over. If this happens on the first pouring, set the plaster mold aside to dry for a few more days.

Instead of making a plaster mold for jigs you can also buy a finished metal mold for pouring jigs. These are reasonable in cost and can be ordered from the mail-order houses listed at the end of chapter 7. Such a metal mold will last forever and will make thousands of jigs.

After the jigs have been poured they require some trimming with cutting pliers and a file. Then you can tie on some bucktail or feathers around the hook to finish the lure. Or you can buy some plastic shrimp or grub tails and put these on the hook. You can also paint the metal head of the jig any color you like. Usually, they are painted white or yellow to match the hair or feathers of the same color on the jig.

Of course, the lures above aren't the only ones you can make yourself. Almost any fishing lure you see or buy can be copied at home. It may not look as perfect as a store-bought lure, but it will catch fish, and, after all, that's all that counts.

# 16. Saltwater Fish

## Bottom Fish

There are many kinds of fish that can be caught by bottom fishing with bait in salt water. You not only catch bottom fish, but also many so-called game fish that usually swim near the surface. The following are some of the more popular fishes taken by bottom fishing.

### FLOUNDERS

There are many kinds of flounders caught in the ocean, but the winter flounder found along the Atlantic coast is the most numerous. The winter flounder, like

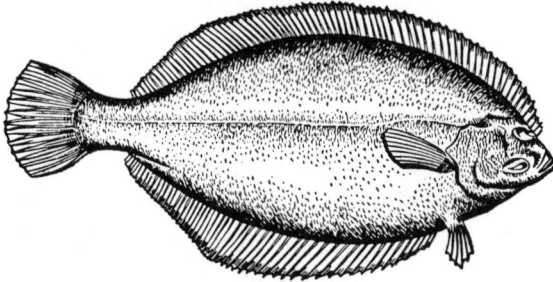

Winter flounder

all flounders, is a thin, flat fish with a brown back and a white belly or undersides. It has two eyes on the top or back side and a small mouth with no teeth. Fish caught are usually between ½ pound and 1 pound in weight, but can reach 5 or 6 pounds.

Winter flounder are found from Canada to North Carolina, but are most plentiful from Massachusetts to New Jersey. These fish like mud or sand bottoms in bays, inlets, and channels. To catch them you use Chestertown or flounder hooks in size No. 7 or 9 baited with small pieces of bloodworm, sandworm, clam, or mussel. The best months for winter-flounder fishing are March, April, May, October, and November.

Another popular flounder is the summer flounder, also known as the fluke. The fluke has a larger mouth than the winter flounder and grows much bigger, sometimes reaching 20 pounds. Most of the fluke caught, however, run from 1 to 5 pounds. They are found along the greater part of the Atlantic coast, but are most numerous from Massachusetts to New Jersey. Fluke fishing is best in the bays, channels, inlets, and up to a mile or two off the beaches in the ocean. Here, where the boats drift with the tide or wind, let the sinker and bait bounce along the bottom. The biggest fluke are usually caught in the deeper water along edges of channels and around sunken wrecks or rocks.

For fluke you use long-shanked hooks, such as the Carlisle, in sizes Nos. 3/0, 4/0, 5/0, and 6/0, depending on the size of the fish running. These are tied on a long, 3-foot leader a few inches above the sinker. The best bait for fluke is a live killifish or some other small baitfish such as a spearing or sand eel. These are usually used with a strip of squid bait on the hook. First add the squid, then the small fish. Sometimes a fluke spinner or two is added above the bait. The best months for fluke fishing are June, July, August, and September.

BLACKFISH

The blackfish, or tautog, is another popular bottom fish caught from Canada to New Jersey. This is a dark, thick fish, with big buckteeth and round lips, usually running from 1 to 5 pounds in weight, but occasionally reaching 20 pounds.

Blackfish are found over rocky bottoms, oyster and mussel beds, and around wrecks and bridge pilings. They also feed around rock jetties and breakwaters. You lose a lot of sinkers and hooks when blackfishing,

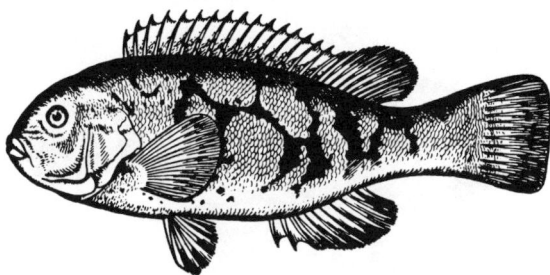

Blackfish

but this can't be avoided if you want to catch them.

To catch blackfish you need a fairly stiff, strong boat rod and Virginia hooks in sizes Nos. 2 to 7, depending on the size of the fish. You can also use Eagle Claw hooks in sizes No. 1/0 or 2/0. One or two hooks should be tied low on the line just above the sinker. For bait you can use a piece of clam, sandworm, or a fiddler crab. Green crabs can also be used if you can get them. Give a blackfish plenty of time to swallow the bait before you set the hook.

SEA BASS

The sea bass is another bottom fish found and caught along the Atlantic coast from Massachusetts to North Carolina. This fish is dark in color and has a big head and mouth. Most sea bass will run from ½ pound to 3 pounds in weight. The larger ones are called humpbacks because of the shape of their backs. These are bluish in color and still darker than the smaller ones.

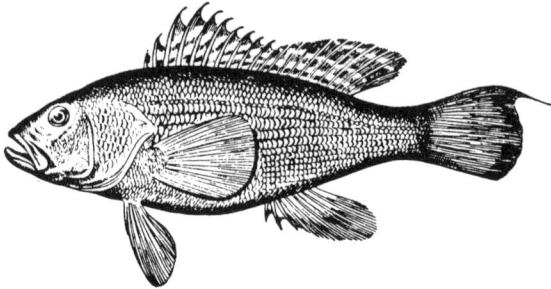

**Sea bass**

Sea bass sometimes reach 8 pounds in weight, and they make good eating.

The smaller sea bass are found in bays, inlets, and close to shore in the ocean. The larger ones are found in deeper water around sunken wrecks or over mussel beds. They also like rocky bottoms, where they can feed on crabs and small fishes.

You can use Eagle Claw hooks in sizes 2/0 or 3/0 for small sea bass and 4/0 or 5/0 for larger ones. The hooks can be baited with a large piece of clam, squid, or baitfish or with a small piece of fish. Sea bass are very greedy and bite quickly as soon as the bait reaches the bottom. They will steal the bait from a hook in a short time, so it pays to reel in after every bite to see if the hooks are still covered with bait.

PORGIES

The porgies are real "panfish of the sea" and, like sunfish in fresh water, they are the most numerous of

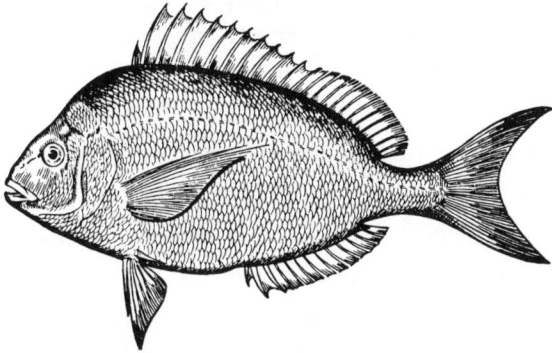

Porgy

bottom fish. The northern porgy is found from Massachusetts to the Carolinas, while other porgies are found in southern waters. The northern porgy, also called the scup, is a deep-bodied fish with large fins and sharp spines. Porgies average about 1 pound in weight and grow to 3 or 4 pounds.

When porgies arrive in the spring around May and June, they come in big schools numbering thousands if not millions of fish. The smaller porgies are caught in bays and inlets near shore, while the larger ones stay in deeper water offshore. They are most numerous around mussel or oyster beds and over rocky bottoms. A line baited with three hooks will often catch them two or three at a time.

They are usually caught on No. 1/0 or 2/0 hooks such as the Eagle Claw, baited with pieces of clam. They will also bite on worms, squid, and shrimp.

Porgies put up a good fight on light tackle, so it's best to use a limber rod for them.

## COD

During the winter months from November to March, the most popular bottom fish caught in the North Atlantic is the codfish. The cod is usually light brown or dirty green in color on its back and has small spots on both sides of its body. The mouth is large, and there is a single whisker on the chin. This is a big fish, usually weighing from 3 to 20 pounds, but often running up to 30, 40, and even 50 pounds in weight. The largest cod caught on rod and reel weighed 98 pounds, and cod can grow to well over 100 pounds.

Codfishing is generally done from an anchored or drifting boat, over rocky or mussel bottoms and around offshore banks or shallower spots. Sometimes cod come close to shore, where they can be caught from piers or jetties.

You need a strong boat rod for codfish because you

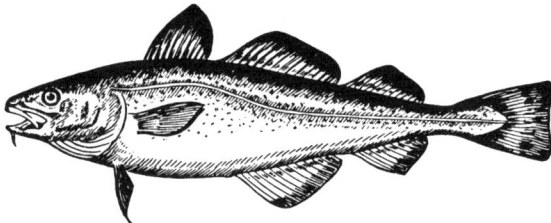

Cod

often use sinkers weighing 10 or 12 ounces or more and large baits on the hooks. Big 7/0 or 8/0 Eagle Claw or Sproat hooks are baited with large pieces of clam or fish for codfish. Cod will also hit a shiny diamond jig worked up and down near the bottom.

## CROAKER

The croaker is a small bottom fish that is very plentiful from Maryland south to the Gulf of Mexico. It is brassy in color and has dark spots on the back and upper fins. This fish gets its name from the croaking sound it makes. The croaker averages about 1 pound in weight, but sometimes reaches 3 pounds.

Croakers are found mostly in bays, inlets, tidal rivers, and along the surf. They like shallow water over grassy or sandy flats. You can catch croakers in the daytime, but some of the best fishing takes place at night. Croakers are caught all year round in southern waters and from June to October in northern waters.

Since it is a small fish it should be caught on light

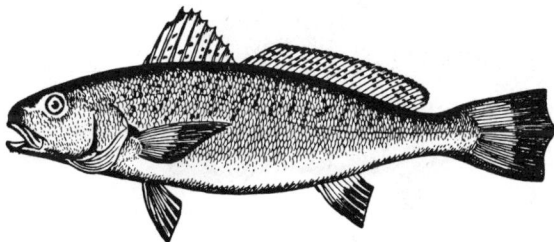

Croaker

tackle for the most sport. A spinning outfit is ideal for this purpose. Use small No. 1/0 or No. 1 hooks baited with sea worms, pieces of clam, squid, shedder crab, or shrimp.

SNAPPERS

In tropical waters one of the largest families of bottom fish are the snappers. At least 250 species are found in the warm waters of the world. Some snappers, such as the red snapper, grow big, often reaching a weight of 20 or 30 pounds. Red snappers are most plentiful in deeper offshore waters on so-called snapper banks. Red snappers are caught only with strong tackle. Use 6/0 to 8/0 hooks baited with small fish or chunks of fish.

Another snapper that is often caught is the mangrove snapper. It gets its name because it is often found around mangrove tree roots. Mangrove snappers are also found around jetties, piers, bridges, and

Mangrove snapper

coral reefs. They don't grow as large as the red snapper, so you can use a smaller hook such as the Eagle Claw No. 2/0, 3/0, or 4/0. Mangrove snappers bite on live shrimp, dead shrimp, small fish, cut mullet, and crabs. They will also often strike artificial lures and so can be caught on plugs, spoons, and jigs.

There are many other snappers, such as the lane snapper, dog snapper, schoolmaster, muttonfish, and yellowtail, which can be caught in the same waters. They can be fished for with the same hooks and baits as those used for mangrove snappers.

GROUPERS

Another large family of bottom fishes in tropical waters are the groupers. There are many different kinds, such as the Nassau grouper, black grouper, yellow grouper, rock grouper, and the red grouper.

Groupers are usually found around coral reefs, rocks, sunken wrecks, and piers and bridges. They are

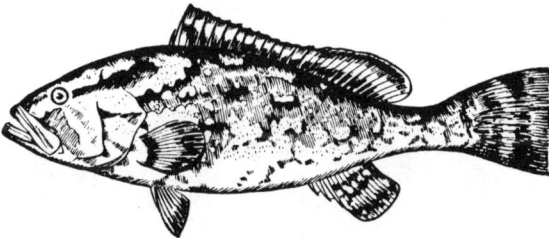

Red grouper

strong fish that often succeed in tangling your line on underwater obstructions and cutting it off, so you need a rather stiff rod and strong line when fishing for them.

Most of the groupers reach a large size and have big mouths, so hooks running from 4/0 to 8/0 can be used. They will bite on live or dead fish such as whole or chunk mullet, grunts, and sardines. Groupers will also take live or dead shrimp when used as bait.

GRUNTS

The grunts are very numerous in warm seas. They do not grow very big, averaging about 1 pound or less in weight, but they are plentiful, and large catches are often made. Some of the grunts that are caught are the margate, the gray grunt, blue-striped grunt, white grunt, French grunt, black margate, yellow grunt, porkfish, and pigfish.

Small No. 1 or 1/0 hooks are used for grunts, and such baits as pieces of shrimp, crab, sea worm, clams, or fish are used. For the most sport, light tackle should be used, and a spinning outfit is ideal.

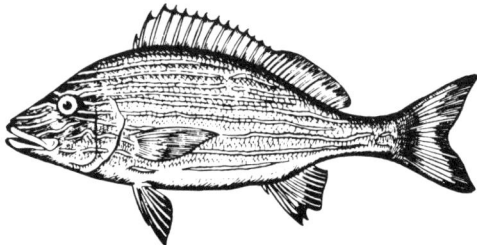

Yellow grunt

OTHER BOTTOM FISH

There are many other bottom fish that can be caught in salt water in the Atlantic and Pacific oceans and in the Gulf of Mexico. Such fish as the spot, or Lafayette; haddock; pollack; silver hake, or whiting, ling, and herring are caught in the Atlantic. In tropical waters you can catch jewfish, sheepshead, pompano, angelfish, and saltwater catfish. In Pacific waters there are the halibut, spotfin croakers, yellowfin croakers, corbina, rockfish, surf perch, lingcod, cabezon, and greenlings.

# Surf Fish

A surf angler must know the best spots to fish along the beaches and rocky shores if he wants to catch anything. The easy way to locate the best fishing spot is to ask a friend or a fishing tackle dealer who knows where the fish have been running recently. If the newspaper in your area has an outdoor column, you can often read where the fish have been biting recently. Down by the beach you can often locate the best fishing spot by looking for other surf anglers who may be catching fish. If you see several surf anglers lined up in one spot, then it's a good idea to try your luck there too. If you can't find out where the fish are biting from other anglers, you must try to locate them yourself. At the beach look for gulls or terns screaming and diving into the water. These birds feed on smaller fish that are chased to the surface by the larger fish. Sometimes you can see the smaller fish leaping out of the water, trying to get away from the larger fish. Or one of the big fish may come up and splash on top of the water.

If you can't see any birds or fish breaking, you must fish in the most likely spots. Usually the best fishing takes place in the deeper holes and channels near shore. You can locate these deeper spots often called sloughs and troughs by looking for blue or dark-green water. Lighter-colored water and white water caused by breaking waves indicate shallower spots. Here you will often find a sandbar, rocky reef, or shallow flat. These spots are often good for striped bass when the water is rough.

One good method of fishing from sandy beaches is to walk along the water's edge and make a cast or two every 50 feet or so with an artificial lure such as a metal squid, spoon, or plug.

Along rocky shores some of the best spots to fish are rocky points and coves. Those areas that have sunken or exposed rocks showing are worth trying. Striped bass like to lie near such rocks, especially when the water is rough.

If there are any jetties or breakwaters, you can try casting from these. Usually the best spot on a jetty is near the front, where you can cast into deep water. But fish such as striped bass and bluefish are often caught in the shallower water near shore and alongside the rocks of the jetty or breakwater.

If there is an inlet or river emptying into the ocean,

this is one of the best spots to fish. Here you will find many surf fish waiting for the smaller baitfish that enter and leave such inlets or rivers. Usually the best time to fish such locations is when the tide is going out.

Just as important as picking the best spot is choosing the best time to go surf-fishing. You'll catch more fish if you go out early in the morning, just as the sun is rising. Another good time to fish is in the evening, when the sun is setting. Many surf anglers also fish at night. This can be a lot of fun when the moon is shining, but fish are also caught on the darkest nights. You need a good headlight or searchlight when fishing at night.

Striped bass are easier to catch when the water is rough than when it is calm and clear. When big waves are rolling in and breaking on shore, you will often find striped bass feeding in the white water. Good surf-fishing is often found right after a storm. However, if the water gets too brown or too dirty with seaweed or debris, the fishing is usually poor. Then you must wait until the water gets clean again to have good fishing.

A good surf angler also knows how to use the lures or baits to get the most bites or strikes. When surf-fishing, you have to watch the waves closely. Wait till a big wave approaches and then cast behind or beyond the wave. As you reel the lure in, vary the speed. Turn the reel handle fast when a wave carries the lure toward you. Turn it slower when the current or backwash pulls the lure away from you.

For bluefish and small striped bass you should reel a metal lure faster than for big striped bass or weakfish. Try to imitate a wounded baitfish with your lure. Surface plugs should be worked fairly fast and jerked at regular intervals to create a splash on top of the water. Underwater plugs should be reeled in at a medium or slow speed. All lures should be reeled more slowly at night than in the daytime. And when the water is calm and clear, fast reeling often produces better results than slow reeling. At all times it pays to change lures until you find one that the fish like.

When the fish refuse to take artificial lures in the surf, you can often catch them on natural baits. You can bait your hook with a piece of mullet, menhaden, or other baitfish, sea worm, crab, squid, or shrimp and cast out as far as you can. Then reel in slowly, letting the bait stay a minute or two in a new spot each time. Keep doing this until the bait is near the beach. Then reel in and cast out again. When you feel a bite, let the fish swallow the bait. When the fish starts to move off, strike hard to set the hook.

The kind of fish you will catch from the surf depends on where you live and fish. The following are the most common and popular surf fish.

STRIPED BASS

The striped bass is caught in the surf along the Atlantic coast from North Carolina to Maine and along the Pacific coast around San Francisco. A striped bass

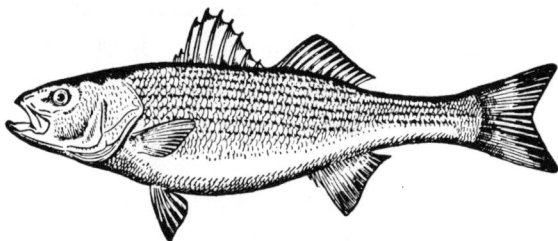

Striped bass

is easily recognized by the seven or eight stripes on its sides. Most of the striped bass you catch will run anywhere from 1 pound or 2 up to 20 pounds in weight. But many fish weighing 30, 40, and 50 pounds are caught.

You can catch striped bass in the surf on a wide variety of lures and baits. They will take metal squids, spoons, plugs, jigs, rigged eels, eelskin lures, and plastic eels and fish. They bite on such natural baits as bloodworms, sandworms, shedder crabs, shrimp, clams, squid, and small fish such as mullet, menhaden, and butterfish. For small striped bass, No. 4/0, 5/0, or 6/0 hooks should be used; for large striped bass, Nos. 7/0, 8/0, and 9/0 hooks are used. The Eagle Claw and O'Shaughnessy patterns are good hooks for bass.

In the surf look for striped bass around rock and wood jetties, breakwaters, and piers. They are often found along rocky shores and sandy beaches. Early in the morning, at dusk, and throughout the night are the best times to catch striped bass. They like rough water and are often caught during and after a storm.

The best striped-bass fishing along the Atlantic coast takes place in the spring and fall. June, September, October, and November are good months.

BLUEFISH

The bluefish is another fish that is often caught in the surf along the Atlantic coast from Cape Cod to Florida. It gets its name from the blue-green color of its back. The bluefish has a large mouth armed with many sharp teeth. Most of the bluefish caught in the surf run from 2 to 6 pounds. However, there are times when larger blues weighing from 6 to 15 pounds appear near the beaches. A few weighing over 20 pounds have been caught by surf anglers. They reach over 30 pounds in weight.

Bluefish are unpredictable fish, and it is difficult to tell when and where they may appear. Some years they disappear entirely along the Atlantic coast. When they are present, they are usually caught in the surf from

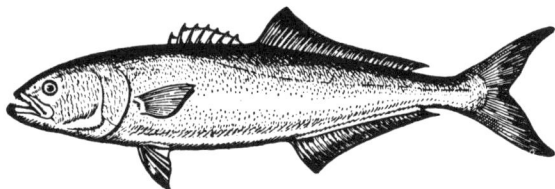

Bluefish

June to October in northern waters and during the winter months in Florida. You can usually locate bluefish, and, of course, other game fish as well, by watching for gulls or terns wheeling and diving excitedly near the beach or shore.

You can catch bluefish on such lures as metal squids, spoons, jigs, or plugs. They also take rigged eels and eelskin lures. They bite on natural baits such as small fish or pieces of fish cut from menhaden, mullet, or butterfish. The hooks should be between Nos. 5/0 and 8/0, depending on the size of the fish running at the time. The Eagle Claw is a favorite hook pattern for the blues. The hooks should be attached to a wire leader since a bluefish's teeth can bite through ordinary lines or leaders.

Bluefish like a fast-moving lure, so when you see them feeding, cast a metal squid or heavy spoon out and reel it in as fast as you can turn the handle.

CHANNEL BASS

The channel bass is a favorite fish with surf anglers from Virginia to the Gulf of Mexico. It is most plentiful along the beaches of Virginia and North Carolina where they are caught from April to November.

Channel bass are large, copper-colored fish with big mouths and heads. At the base of the tail there is a black spot. Channel bass usually run from 10 to 30 pounds in the surf, but big fish up to 50 and 60 pounds are sometimes caught.

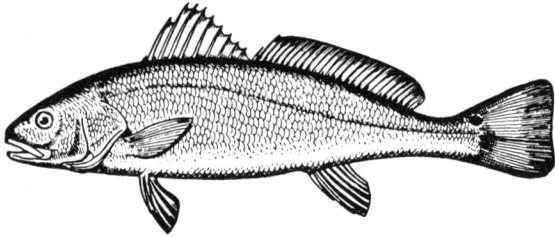

Channel bass

You can catch channel bass with the same surf-fishing rods and reels used for striped bass. They also take the same lures, such as metal squids, spoons, plugs, and jigs. But most surf-fishing for channel bass is done with natural baits such as pieces of mullet, menhaden, squid, shrimp, or crab. For small channel bass, called puppy drum, you can use hooks in sizes from 4/0 to 6/0. For big fish, hooks in sizes 7/0, 8/0, and 9/0 are used.

When found in the surf, the channel bass prefer the sandbars, holes, and channels or troughs. Sometimes they can be seen chasing menhaden or other small fish, but most of the time you have to cast out to a likely spot and let the bait lie there. Give the channel bass plenty of time to take the bait before trying to set the hook.

The best months for channel-bass fishing along the Atlantic coast are April, May, October, and November. In Florida the winter months are often good. Fish for channel bass early in the morning and in the evening for best results.

WEAKFISH

There are two kinds of weakfish caught by surf anglers along the Atlantic coast. One is the common, or northern, weakfish, which is found from Cape Cod to Florida. The other is the spotted, or southern, weakfish, which is often called the sea trout in southern waters. The southern weakfish is found from Virginia to the Gulf of Mexico. The two kinds of weakfish have similar body shapes, but the northern weakfish is

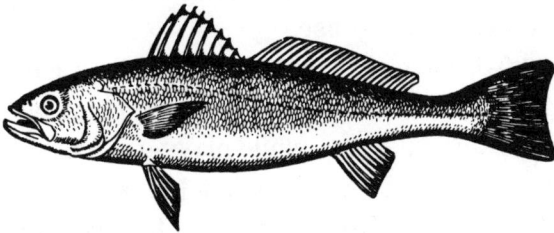

common weakfish

spotted weakfish

Two kinds of weakfish

more colorful, having a variety of colors along its back and sides and orange or yellow fins. The southern weakfish is mostly silvery, with black spots scattered along the back and sides. Most weakfish run from 1 to 5 pounds in weight. But occasionally big fish up to 10 or 12 pounds may appear in the surf. The northern weakfish grows up to 20 pounds in weight, while the southern weakfish reaches 15 pounds.

Weakfish are caught casting in the surf with such artificial lures as metal squids, spoons, jigs, and small plugs. They are also caught with live baits such as sandworms, squid, shrimp, shedder crab, and pieces of mullet or other fish. Hooks Nos. 3/0, 4/0, 5/0, and 6/0 are the best sizes to use.

Weakfish have that name because they have weak mouths that tear easily. Use your lightest tackle for these fish and take care while playing them on the end of a line. Always use a gaff or a net to land a good-sized weakfish. Only the small ones (up to 1 pound) should be lifted into a boat or on shore.

Weakfish can be caught during the day or night. Along the beaches, fish at high tide and when it is going out. Jetties and breakwaters can be fished at low tide if there is deep water near the end.

## WHITING

The whiting is a small fish caught in the surf along the Atlantic coast and in the Gulf of Mexico. Two kinds are usually caught: the northern whiting, found from Massachusetts to Florida and often called the kingfish,

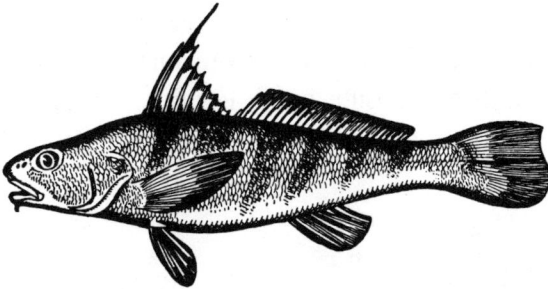

Northern whiting

and the southern whiting, found from Virginia to Florida. Both kinds of whiting have small underslung mouths and vary in color from gray to black with faint stripes on the sides.

Since whiting average about 1 pound and rarely reach more than 5 or 6 pounds, light fishing tackle is most suitable for them. A medium-weight surf spinning outfit is ideal. Whiting are caught mostly on live baits such as bloodworms, sand bugs, bits of clam or squid, or pieces of shrimp. These are placed on small hooks such as the No. 1/0 Eagle Claw.

Whiting give a very rapid, sharp bite, which you feel as a series of sharp tugs. You should strike back immediately to set the hook; if you wait too long your bait will be stolen.

OTHER SURF FISH

There are many other kinds of fish that can be caught by surf-fishing. In northern Atlantic waters anglers catch blackfish, or tautog; pollock; croakers; and flounders. In waters around Florida they catch pompano, jack crevalle, snook, tarpon, snappers, and grouper. In California they catch corbina, croakers, surf perch, rockfish, and occasional halibut.

## Game Fish

The following are the most important game fish caught in offshore waters.

### SWORDFISH

The swordfish is an offshore fish that most big-game anglers would like to catch. However, these deep-sea fighters are not plentiful, and they are hard to hook. Even after you do hook a swordfish, you stand a good chance of losing him when he breaks the line or the hook pulls out of his mouth. Many anglers have fought a swordfish for several hours, only to lose him in the end.

Swordfish

The swordfish is easily recognized by its broad bill, tall dorsal fin, and wide tail. The average swordfish caught on rod and reel runs from 100 to 400 pounds. But in some spots, such as the Pacific Ocean off South America, swordfish weighing anywhere from 500 to over 1,000 pounds are caught.

Swordfish are found in many parts of the world, including both the Atlantic and Pacific coasts of the United States. The best fishing days have little wind and calm water. At such times you can often spot swordfish fins above the water. Then the captain of the boat trolls a whole squid or fairly large fish, such as a mackerel, in front of the fish, as bait. Most times the swordfish refuse to take the bait, but every so often one will hit it and swallow it, and then the fight begins. If you are lucky and the fish is hooked securely, you may land your swordfish in two or three hours. But if the fish is not hooked properly or is very big, you may have to fight it most of the day.

Swordfish have also been caught at night by drifting with baits, such as squid or whole fish, down deep.

## MARLIN

Marlin are another big-game fish that are caught offshore. There are three kinds of marlin caught in the United States: the white marlin, which is the smallest; the striped marlin, which is larger; and the blue marlin, which is the biggest. They all have spears, or bills, and broad tails. The white marlin and blue marlin are found

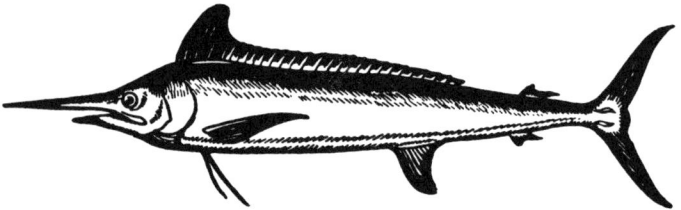

White marlin

along the Atlantic coast, while the striped marlin is found in Pacific waters.

Marlin are caught by trolling baits or lures well off-shore. At one time, only whole natural baits such as mullet, mackerel, ballyhoo, flying fish, and bonito were trolled on top for marlin. But in recent years more and more of these fish have been caught on plastic lures made to imitate squid or small fish.

Marlin are supposed to hit natural baits with their bills; then they return and take the bait into their mouths. That is why outriggers are useful when fishing for marlin. The slack line allows the fish time to swallow the bait. Then, when the line tightens, the rod is brought back hard to set the hook. This "drop-back" is used mostly with natural baits. When using lures, the marlin hit fast and hard and get hooked immediately.

Marlin often jump out of the water or "tail walk" along the surface when hooked. They fight long and hard, and it may take up to two or three hours to land a big fish. However, most white marlin rarely go over 100 pounds, and such fish can usually be landed in less than an hour. Striped marlin and blue marlin may run several hundred pounds in weight and take more time to land.

SAILFISH

The sailfish looks somewhat like a marlin, but has a slimmer body and a large, fanlike dorsal fin that gives it its name. There are two kinds of sailfish—the Atlantic sailfish, found mostly off Florida, and the Pacific sailfish, found off Mexico and Lower California. The Atlantic sailfish rarely reaches more than 100 pounds, but the Pacific sailfish often grows considerably larger.

Sailfish are caught trolling in the same way as marlin with whole small mullet, or ballyhoo, or with fish strips. They are also caught by fishing with live baits

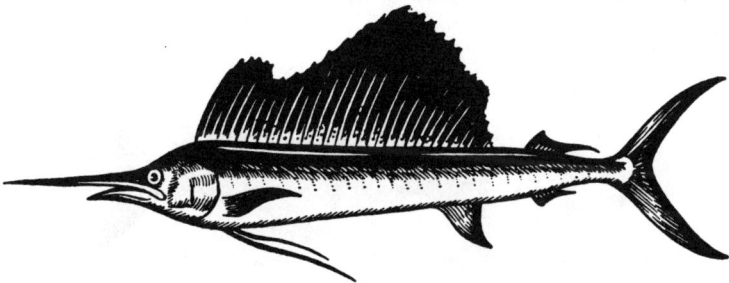

**Sailfish**

such as blue runners. And they will hit plastic lures.

Sailfish are more plentiful than marlin or other big-game fish found in offshore waters. You can charter a boat in Florida for a half day or full day and stand a good chance of hooking one. When a sailfish is hooked he leaps out of the water many times before being boated. Most sailfish are not eaten, but are released alive in the water to live and fight another day. Unless you catch your first sailfish or a really big one. Then you may want to have it mounted.

TUNA

The bluefin tuna is a popular fish with offshore anglers, since it reaches a good size and fights very hard on the end of a line. Tuna are also good to eat and have been caught in nets and harpooned so much that there are few of these fish left in the ocean.

The smaller bluefin tuna, under 100 pounds, are called school tuna; the larger tuna reaching over that weight and up to 1,000 pounds or more are called giant tuna.

Tuna

Bluefin tuna are found in both the Pacific and Atlantic oceans. Hooking and landing a giant tuna is not easy. These big tuna are found in only a few spots, and they do not always take a bait. The smaller school tuna, however, are easier to fool and more plentiful. The larger tuna are usually caught on whole live or dead fish such as herring, mackerel, whiting, or menhaden. The smaller school tuna are caught by trolling feather lures, jigs, metal lures, or plastic lures.

When a good-sized tuna is hooked it takes off many yards of line at a fast speed, not only once but many times. A school tuna under 100 pounds can be landed in an hour or less, but a giant tuna may fight longer.

OTHER GAME FISH

Many other fish, such as dolphin, albacore, bonito, are caught in offshore waters. In southern waters one can also catch barracuda, amberjack, wahoo, king mackerel, and sharks.

Offshore fishing also offers the possibility of seeing such big sea creatures as turtles, porpoises, or, perhaps, if you're lucky, a whale.

# 17. Care and Repair of Fishing Tackle

Fishing tackle can be expensive if you have to buy a new rod, reel, line, or lure very often. However, by taking proper care of your fishing tackle, you can make it last a long time. You can also save money by repairing your own rods, reels, and lures.

The fiberglass or graphite rods used today require little care in order to remain in good condition. After each fishing trip, especially in salt water, the entire fishing rod should be wiped with a rag soaked in fresh water and then dried with a dry rag. The metal parts, such as the guides, ferrules, and reel seats, should then be wiped with an oily rag. If you do this regularly you will find that the metal parts on the fishing rod will not corrode.

At the beginning of each fishing season, the fishing rod should be examined carefully. The heat and dryness of heated rooms and apartments will often loosen the ferrules, reel seat, or top guide on a fishing rod. These can be made tight by heating the metal parts over a gas stove or alcohol lamp or even electric stove. First you should remove the ferrule or reel seat from the rod and heat it over a flame or other heat until it is very hot. You can use pliers or gloves to hold the metal part so you won't burn your hands. Then take a stick of ferrule cement and heat it over the flame until it melts. (You can buy this ferrule cement in any fishing tackle store.) Now spread the soft cement over the part of the fishing rod where the metal part fitted originally. Do this while holding the rod high over the flame or heat so that the cement remains in a liquid state. Then force the ferrule or reel seat back into place. If it doesn't go on easily, hold it over the flame and then push it on. There are also ferrule cements on the market that do not have to be heated. They are like most cements or glues and come in tubes in a liquid state. All you have to do is squeeze some on the rod and inside the ferrule and join them together.

If there is a lot of space between the reel seat or

ferrule and the wooden part of the rod where it fits, you may have to add a filler. The best material for this is a few strands of a thread such as soft bread cord fitted over the wood as shown in the illustration below. Then smear on the ferrule cement as before, and force the ferrule or reel seat into place.

If any of the guides on your rod are loose, they should be removed, or if the windings holding the guides are old and worn, you can remove them all. This is done by cutting the old windings or wrappings with a razor blade or sharp knife. Then you can peel them off and remove the guides. The next step is to take off the old varnish by rubbing the rod with fine steel wool.

The rod is now ready for winding, for which you can use nylon rod-winding thread, which comes in different sizes and colors. For light, thin, freshwater fishing rods, a No. A winding thread is best. For the heavier, thicker, saltwater rods a No. D winding thread is bet-

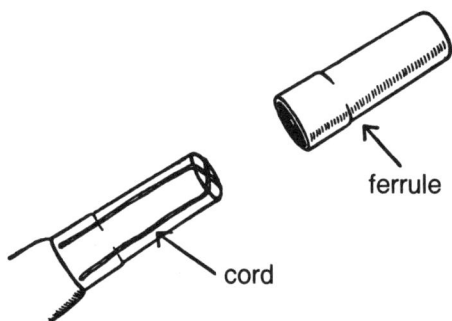

ferrule

cord

Cord on rod to insure tight fit of ferrule

ter. The only real trick to winding a rod is to start and finish it properly. To start the winding, tuck the end of the thread under the first few turns until it is buried. (See *A* in next drawing.) Then continue wrapping until you are ready to finish. Stop a few turns from the end and take a short piece of the thread, form a loop, and place it over the end of the winding. The loop should face out past the last winding on the rod. (See *B.*) Then make several more turns of thread over the loop. Next take the end of the winding thread and run it through the eye of the loop *(C)*. Finally, take the two ends of the buried loop and pull the end of the winding under the last few turns. This buries the end of the thread under the winding *(D)*.

After the winding is completed, take a comb or a round piece of smooth plastic and rub the windings to flatten the thread and close up any spaces between the strands. Now get some color preservative and apply it

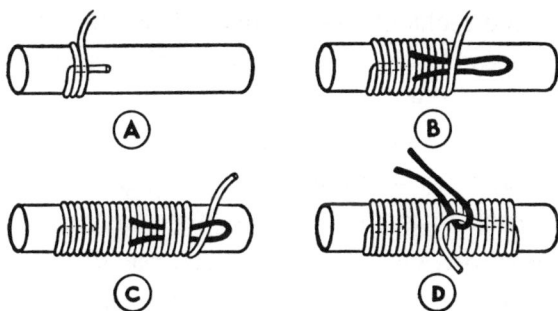

Winding a rod

over the nylon windings. You can buy a small bottle of this preservative in any fishing tackle store. Two or three coats should be applied, allowing each to dry first. This is done to preserve the true colors of the thread when varnish is applied over the thread.

Some anglers varnish the entire fishing rod, but with fiberglass or graphite or Boron rods you need only to apply the varnish on the windings. Buy a small jar of rod varnish and give the windings two or three coats, allowing time for each coat to dry before applying another coat.

Fishing reels also require some care if you want to avoid trouble later. After each fishing trip it's a good idea to wipe the reel with a damp rag. This is especially important with saltwater reels. Some anglers even thoroughly wash their reels in fresh water after using them in salt water. Then the reel should be wiped until it is completely dry. After the reel is dry it can be wiped with an oil-soaked rag. Then oil and grease the moving parts of the reel and any opening where the lubricants are required. Reels should also be oiled and greased before each fishing trip.

Once or twice a year you can give your reel a thorough cleaning by washing it in kerosene. To do this get a stiff brush to get into the corners and tight spots. First, however, you should take the reel apart so that the working parts are exposed. Then wipe the reel dry, and oil and grease the moving parts thoroughly.

If your fishing reel is not working properly, or requires a major overhaul, it can be taken to a local fishing tackle store that does such work. Or you can send the reel to the factory for a complete checkup and repairs. The best time to do this is during the winter months, when you don't need the reel and the factory has plenty of time to do a good job.

Fishing lines require less care than rods and reels, since nowadays most of them are made from synthetic materials that do not rot. However, fly-casting lines do require more care, especially during the winter months. Do not leave the fly line on the fishing reel, but coil it loosely in a large cardboard box or wind it around a large cylindrical object such as a section of a wide tube. Before you do this, wash the line in clean fresh water, then dress it with the special fly dressing sold in most fishing tackle stores.

Other fishing lines, such as braided lines and monofilament lines, can be left on the reel, but even here it is a good idea to wash the line first with clean fresh water, especially if it has been used in salt water. It is also a good idea to examine the first few feet of any line to see if it is badly worn or frayed. If it looks weak, cut off the bad section. If the line on your reel is too short to fill the reel spool properly, you can put some old fishing line under the good line as backing. Or you can remove the old line and replace it with a new one.

Fishing lures require a great deal of care and repair, especially if they are used in salt water. The hooks and other metal parts rust or corrode. Paint on wooden plugs tends to chip or crack. The finishes on spoons and spinners corrode or tarnish.

If a wooden plug is slightly chipped or cracked, it can be touched up with quick-drying enamel paint or lacquer and a small brush, but if it is badly cracked or chipped it must be repainted completely. First, sandpaper the plug to remove some of the old paint and make it rough. Then paint the plug with white enamel or lacquer. It may need two or three coats of white paint to cover the old paint and wood thoroughly. After the white paint is dry you can add other colors in various combinations. Instead of painting the plugs with a brush, you'll do a quicker and often better job using one of those pressure spray cans of color that can be bought in any hardware store.

Spoons and spinners, if tarnished or corroded, can be made bright and shiny by washing them in soap and lukewarm water and then polishing them with a metal polish and a cloth.

If the feathers or bucktail hair wound around any of the hooks or jigs or spoons is badly worn, it can be cut off with a razor blade or knife. Then tie new feathers or hair around the hook.

Hooks that are badly rusted should be replaced with new ones. Make sure you get the same size. If the hooks are only slightly rusted, they can be cleaned with steel wool or emery cloth and then wiped with an oily rag. You can also paint the hooks to keep them from rusting too quickly.

Check also the points and barbs on all your hooks. Make sure the points are sharp and not bent or broken. If any hooks are dull they should be sharpened with a small file or sharpening stone.

Taking care of your fishing tackle may seem like a lot of trouble. But it is important to make sure your fishing tackle is in good condition at all times. You never know when you will hook a big fish, and if any part of your tackle is weak you may lose him.

# 18. Sportsmanship

Fishing is a sport that has very few rules or regulations. Other sports, such as baseball, basketball, tennis, and golf, for example, have to be played under strict official rules. But fishing has no such official rules, and you are free to fish in any way you please.

However, there are some unwritten laws that are practiced and observed by most anglers who try to be good sports. The main reason for going fishing is to have fun. At the same time, a good sport doesn't interfere with another angler's fishing. Because more and more people are fishing today, the popular spots are usually crowded, especially so on weekends and holidays. But a few rules of behavior will make fishing a pleasure even in crowded spots.

Always remember, for example, that when fishing a trout stream, the angler who arrives first at a certain pool or section of the stream is entitled to fish that spot without being crowded. This is especially true if the pool is small. If an angler can reach almost every section of the pool with a cast, then there is room for only one trout angler. If the pool is long or wide, there may be room for more than one angler. But anglers should be able to stand a good distance away from each other. In some streams anglers stand shoulder to shoulder, especially when the fishing season has just opened; but this isn't real fly-fishing and most expert anglers avoid such spots. There are usually several good pools or fishing spots in a trout stream. If a spot is taken or crowded, walk down to the next one.

The same holds true for surf-fishing. If an angler is already fishing, stay at least 50 or even 100 feet away. Even if the surf angler is catching fish, it is bad manners to crowd him. A surf angler needs plenty of room to cast in a wide arc and to fight a hooked fish. If you are too close the angler may lose a hooked fish that tangles in your line.

Crowding should also be avoided when you are fishing from a boat. If anglers are anchored over a fishing spot, be sure you are at least 50 feet from them when you drop your anchor. If they are casting lures or trolling, you should stay at least 150 to 300 feet away from them.

Never cut across the lines of a trolling boat. Wait until the boat passes and is at least 300 feet away before moving in behind it. Otherwise you may entangle their lines with your propeller and cut them off.

If you are fishing from a boat, don't come so close to shore that anglers on the bank can reach you with a cast. You can move all over the lake, river, or ocean, but the angler on shore is limited to a few spots. Why spoil the sport and endanger yourself and the occupants of your boat by coming so close that a sinker or lure cast from shore can reach you, possibly injuring someone?

Always be careful of the other anglers near you, whether you are casting from shore, a pier, bridge, or jetty. Make sure that no one is behind you when you cast. Always use an overhead cast when casting from a boat or pier. If casting is not allowed on the pier or boat you are fishing from, a sporting angler abides by the rules.

When fishing from a crowded pier or party boat, let out your line as straight as possible so it does not tangle with the lines of the other anglers. Many tangles are not caused by anglers, but by the current, tide, wind, or movement of the boat or hooked fish. If lines do get tangled, try to help untangle them as soon as possible. And if you tangle with another angler's line, don't blame him, even if it is his fault. The next time *you* may be to blame!

A good sport obeys all the fish laws regarding open seasons, size limits, and bag limits. Don't try to fish without a fishing license if you are at an age or in a state that requires such a license. These licenses provide the money used to improve the fishing in a lake or stream. If there were no fishing licenses, there would be fewer fish and fewer spots in which to catch them.

If the law says that you should throw back all fish under a certain size, don't try to keep the small fish. If you are allowed to keep only a certain number of bass or trout, don't try to sneak any extra fish home. And if the season is closed on a certain kind of fish, don't try to catch them. If you do catch one by accident, remove the hook carefully and throw the fish back into the water.

Many fish in fresh and salt water are now protected so that you can keep only a certain number. But others, especially in salt water can be taken in any quantities. Some anglers bring them home by the bagful. If the fish are very plentiful, no harm is done. But if the fish are thrown away without being eaten, the waste is unsporting and poor conservation. If you take too many fish or keep too many small ones, then you are reducing the number of fish that can be caught in the coming years. Most anglers would rather catch one big fish than several smaller ones. So throw back the small fish, and give them a chance to grow up into worthwhile trophies.

Fishing clubs are usually the centers of good sportsmanship. If you enjoy fishing you will probably enjoy the friendliness of a fishing club. You will meet other anglers, some of whom are experts. They are always glad to advise and help beginners. Many fishing clubs hold casting classes and fishing contests to improve your skill. They also have instruction classes for tying flies, making lures and rods. They provide pleasant companions to take along on a fishing trip. Joining a fishing club is usually the quickest and happiest way to become a good angler.

Good fishing to you!

# Index